HEALING LIFE'S
BROKEN DREAMS

HEALING LIFE'S *BROKEN* DREAMS

A Son's Tragedy, a Mother's Grief, a Miracle of Recovery

Patricia Forbes

iUniverse, Inc.
New York Lincoln Shanghai

HEALING LIFE'S *BROKEN* DREAMS
A Son's Tragedy, a Mother's Grief, a Miracle of Recovery

iUniverse books may be ordered through booksellers or by contacting:

iUniverse
2021 Pine Lake Road, Suite 100
Lincoln, NE 68512
www.iuniverse.com
1-800-Authors (1-800-288-4677)

Cover design by Ursula Kur-Sissons

ISBN-13: 978-0-595-35413-9 (pbk)
ISBN-13: 978-0-595-80420-7 (cloth)
ISBN-13: 978-0-595-79909-1 (ebk)
ISBN-10: 0-595-35413-0 (pbk)
ISBN-10: 0-595-80420-9 (cloth)
ISBN-10: 0-595-79909-4 (ebk)

Printed in the United States of America

This book is dedicated in memory of Louis, my son and soul mate,
Who will forever hold my heart…

A Special Dedication

To my sisters, Michele and Gloria, my brother Kenny, my sister-in-law Joanie, and my brothers-in-law Kevin and Jamey, for your love, support, and concern; for picking me up every time I fell; for understanding my pain; for never rushing me to "get on with my life;" and for waiting patiently for me to grieve and become the person I am now. I will love you all forever for all that you have been through with me and for pushing your own devastating grief aside to be at my side.

To my mother, Gloria Forbes, who is the rarest combination of practical, moral, and spiritual and is the least selfish person I have ever known. She has such a strong, sympathetic nature that all those around her seem to find comfort. Through her endless love and strength, she helped me endure the worst tragedy of my life, then taught me how to survive it.

To my father, Kenneth Forbes, for giving me his gift of writing.

To my boyfriend, Tony Alessi, who lived my nightmare, walked the path of grief and sorrow with me, and never gave up hope. Thank you for bringing me back from darkness to light. I will always love you more today than yesterday and less than tomorrow.

And finally to "Lucky" who found me when I needed him the most.

Acknowledgments

I would like to thank the following people for their love, support, friendship, concern, and understanding; and for always giving me a shoulder to lean on and helping me through the most difficult and tragic event in my life. I have been so very blessed to have all of you in my life. Please know how much I appreciated every kind word and gesture, and especially your happiness when I reached the point of survival.

To Stephanie, Kerri, Nick, Jeff, Jen, Barbara, Joanne, Mary, Terry, Fred, Jody, Andrea, Marlene, Robin, Michelle, David, Scott, Marilyn, Bobby, Ciampi, Ronnie, Paul, Lenny, Lynn, Laurie, Johnniemae, to my princess Nicole, to everyone in the Framingham-Brockton office, to the technicians, and especially to my friends at the learning center in Marlboro…who never forgot.

To David Consigli, director of the Consigli-Ruggerio funeral home, for his support, caring, sensitivity, and professionalism during my time of grief and for remaining a true friend.

To my aunts, my uncles, my cousins and their wives, my nephews, and my niece for their understanding, compassion, and acceptance of the "new me" as if they had known her forever.

To Doctor Darrolyn Lindsey, who understood my pain.

To Tony's family for their compassion and understanding and for standing by me while their father, brother, and uncle went through *his* worst nightmare.

A very special acknowledgment to my cousin Lynn-Marie Carty for her encouragement, support, love, and inspiration. Without her this book never would have been written. She will always be my "angel in disguise."

To Katherine Bain owner of Body Image for her generiosity, suggestions and especially her friendship.

To Karen Jackson who was always there for Louis when he needed her.

To Rusty Fischer for his input, his sensitivity to the contents of the book, his patience, and for his faith in me every step of the way. I am truly grateful for what we did together.

To Brett Hacksley and all of Louis friends for being in his life.

A special thank you to Ursula Kur-Sissons for the time and hard work she spent designing the cover of my book.

To her husband Michael, "Today is Mine" is for you.

Contents

Prologue

✦

November 23, 1998

"It's only when we truly know and understand that we have a limited time on earth—and that we have no way of knowing when our time is up—that we will begin to live each day to the fullest, as if it was the only one we had."

—*Elisabeth Kübler-Ross*

There was no premonition; no waking dream. Far from it—that day started out like any other Monday. I woke up wishing I could add one more day to the weekend and sleep in. My alarm went off at 5:00 AM, my usual time to run. It was cold and windy, a typical New England day.

I dragged myself out of bed, slipped into my running clothes, ran for two miles, and came home to my usual routine of grabbing a cup of coffee, taking a shower, washing my hair, putting on my makeup, and dressing for work.

Like I said, it was a day like all the rest.

Except—it wasn't.

That day I was taking two classes for my job, and, unlike most days, where I was running around to gain time, I actually had a little time to spare before going to work, so I did some laundry and picked up the house a little bit. While I drove to Marlboro, where I would be attending class that day, I suddenly remembered that I hadn't told my son, Louis, that I would be late coming home, and I made a mental note to call him sometime that morning.

I was feeling very anxious that day, the first small inkling that something was not quite right in the universe. It wasn't exactly doom and gloom. Not yet, anyway. In fact, I couldn't explain the feeling, but I just didn't feel like myself. I put the radio on and tried to get in a better mood and feel more relaxed, but I just couldn't shake the feeling deep in the pit of my stomach.

Once I got to class, the day went by quickly, but on the way home I remembered that I still hadn't called my son. It might not seem like such a big deal, but we talked on the phone at least once a day.

No matter where he was or what he was doing, Louis would always call just to say hi, or if he needed something. We had been alone so long that we had become very close and *extremely* protective of each other.

We'd weathered a lot over the years: the terrible twos, the darling fours, his awkward preteens, and the rebellious teen years; but now Louis was twenty-one and had just started working for a small construction company.

He seemed fairly happy.

Like I said, it was just a regular old Monday. After class, as on most workdays, I went directly to the gym and did my usual workout of weights and cardio. I spent some time talking to a few friends, and left the gym to go home.

Leaving the gym, the undercurrent that I had sensed all day remained. It was there, slow and steady, flying just below my radar but popping up from time to time to make me feel awkward, unbalanced, and anxious.

I still had a very uneasy feeling that something wasn't right.

I finally got home at 6:30, and as I started walking up the stairs, I saw my caller ID flashing next to the phone. I checked the numbers; all of them were anonymous, but I knew one of them had to be Louis checking in and wondering why I wasn't home at 5:00—and most likely mad that he didn't know where I was.

I retrieved the messages, only to find that there were four, all from Louis, starting from 5:00 and going until 6:15. He hadn't left a call-back number, just messages telling me he would call back, so I took a shower, read the paper, and went through the mail.

It wasn't easy; I was restless. The uneasy feeling wouldn't go away. I couldn't put my finger on it, which only made it all the more frustrating. I tried filling my time to drive it away. Still, there it lurked, just out of sight.

At 7:30 that fateful Monday night, Louis finally called back. He asked the usual questions: where I had been, why I was late, and so on. I told him I was sorry I had forgotten to call him, and let it go.

He was a good boy and a protective son, but sometimes it irritated me when he was like this. I used to feel like I was talking to a boyfriend and not my son, but then I flipped the script onto myself. I had to admit that I acted the same way when I couldn't reach him for one reason or another, so how could I complain?

It's what I had taught him, after all—it's you and me against the world, kid—so eventually we both got used to it. Louis said he was at his boss's house; they had just had a party for one of his friends, and he wanted me to pick him up. He was only a few miles away, so I asked him to be ready and told him that I'd be there in ten minutes. I threw on a pair of sweat pants, some sneakers, and a coat over my nightgown.

As I was leaving, I wondered why he had called me five times instead of just asking one of his friends to take him home. It was the kind of thought you have a million times a day, blink twice, and then it's gone. But the thought still nagged at me; if he'd just asked one of his friends, he'd have been home by now.

The road his boss lived on was a main road, very busy, but well-lit. I put my blinker on, pulled over to the white line on the side, and stopped directly under a streetlight. I looked in my rearview mirror and was glad to see there were no cars coming up the road.

When I looked over to see if Louis was waiting on the porch, I was relieved to see him standing there waiting for me. He had on the new blue flannel shirt and dungarees I had bought him over the weekend on one of our shopping trips together and he was holding his black leather jacket over his shoulder with one hand.

He was just standing there, smiling at me.

It was a brief moment, a flicker in time, but in the rearview mirror of my perception it seems frozen in time. His smile, the buttons on his flannel shirt, those new jeans, which were too crisp for him and needed a dozen more good washes before they'd be quite right. The leather jacket was slung over his shoulder just so—the way guys did in catalogs or movies. My boy, so handsome, so protective, so loving—who could be angry for having to head out at 7:30 at night to pick him up?

All of a sudden, the wind seemed to stop. It was so quiet, as if the entire world had stopped for that brief moment in time. Suddenly I started to feel anxious again. I couldn't breathe. The car got quiet, so quiet I could almost hear the blood pumping in my ears. I looked in my rearview mirror once more and was dismayed to see that cars were now coming up the street.

One set of headlights.

Two.

Then three, until it seemed as if someone had opened a floodgate.

At the same time, almost as if he'd been waiting for his cue, Louis started running toward the car. I watched him in slow motion, like something in a movie: one foot, then the other.

Down one step, then the next.

Across the lawn.

Onto the road.

As he ran, he shifted the leather jacket under his arm, like a running back in the NFL cradles his football. His smile stayed fixed, the brash, confident, knowing smile of youth. "Look, Mom," his smile seemed to scream. "Here I come. Nothing can happen to me. Not today, not ever…"

Only, mothers know better.

I tried to open the door. I couldn't find the handle. I couldn't move. I felt like I wasn't even there. I couldn't do anything except wait, because I knew what was happening.

In many ways, I had known all day…

1

The Beginning

"When I stopped seeing my mother with the eyes of a child, I saw the woman who helped me give birth to myself."

—Nancy Friday

I grew up in a small Massachusetts town called Hopedale. When I say small, I'm not just being quaint. At the time I was born, the population of Hopedale was around four thousand hearty northern souls. (Come to think of it, that number probably hasn't changed all that much in the intervening years.)

I was a twin, and while my sister's name was Michele, everyone always called her by her nickname, "Mike." When my mother found out she was having twins, she and my father decided to call us Pat and Mike (after the Spencer Tracy movie), whether we were two boys or two girls or one of each.

So on December 26, 1952, Pat and Mike were born. My sister arrived first, and I followed a full sixty seconds later. Don't think for one minute that I ever stopped reminding her that she was the older sister. (I still do.)

We were not identical twins; I had blond hair and blue eyes, and Mike had brown hair and brown eyes. We had a brother named Kenny who was four years older than us, so, when we were born, he became the official big brother, a title he relished and lived up to as often as possible.

The first five years of my life we all lived with my grandmother. Next to the phrase "had her hands full" in most modern dictionaries, you can see a picture of my mother, for whom I think this term was officially coined.

In fact, Mom was so busy she would tie us to a tree outside in the summer time, just to let us get some fresh air and play together. But Mom's respite was always short-lived. Before too long, the neighbors would be calling my mother every day to tell her we had taken off our diapers and were running around naked.

To this day I don't know why the local "neighborhood watch" was so concerned about two little girls going *au natural* in the Massachusetts summertime. I mean, really, how far could we run with a rope tied firmly around our waists? And as for indecency, we were only two years old, so what was there to see?

Mike and I slept in the same crib for the first three years before we finally graduated to big-girl beds. Legend has it that my father's mother babysat for us one night, and without thinking, put us in two separate cribs when it was time for bed. We cried and cried, and my poor grandmother couldn't get us to fall asleep, until finally she put us back in the same crib, and once there, we fell fast asleep.

When we were four years old, my parents bought a piece of land in Hopedale. They contracted out a lot of the work, but my mother was always taking us over to the house to play. Meanwhile, Hopedale's hardest working woman painted, wallpapered, stained, and designed our bedroom by herself.

She had my uncle build a hutch with double desks, built-in drawers for our clothes, and a vanity in the middle of each side, and then she added twin beds to make the effect complete. At the time we just thought the room was cool, but later we realized that all of this was done so we would consider ourselves individuals with our own space, even though we were together.

Lest you think Mom was a housewife filling her idle time with hobbies and frills, my mother worked in a bank forty hours every week in addition to caring for the three of us. Meanwhile, my father worked two jobs in order to build the house of their dreams.

Our "dream house" sat on almost two acres of land, and the last half-acre was all woods, so we had a lot of privacy in the backyard. My father helped me build a tree house that became my own private hideaway. The house was brick, with two fireplaces, hardwood floors, and three spacious bedrooms. At that time, it was considered one of the nicest houses in Hopedale. Long before anyone had ever thought of shows like *Trading Spaces* and *While You Were Out,* my parents worked hard at their jobs all week, then, during their so-called free time, they would work in the house until a particular project was complete or they collapsed—whichever came first.

At the age of five, Mike and I entered kindergarten at a Catholic school in Milford and had nuns as teachers. As one might expect, we were not very happy going to school. Gone were the diaper-free days of summer and worse yet, the nuns kept trying to separate my sister and me, but we stayed together as much as possible.

I remember my mother telling us that the nuns would always call her and admonish her to cut our hair. At the time we both had long hair, which my mother braided every morning, but, by the time we came home, the elastics would be out of our hair and we looked like wild children with our hair all over the place. My mother finally cut it, and apparently that made the nuns happy.

We finally left my grandmother's house and moved to our new home in Hopedale, where we would start first grade. Mike and I were eager to explore our new digs, and set off on foot the first chance we had.

I can clearly remember my sister and me walking up the street, where there was a pretty house with a stone wall. Because it was only three houses away from us, we safely crossed the street and started walking atop the stone wall. Out of nowhere came this cute boy with blond hair and blue eyes. He watched us for a while, then came over and said, "You can't walk on that stone wall; it's mine."

My twin and I looked at each other knowingly, and I said, "We can do anything we want because we are older than you."

He looked at us as if he didn't believe we were older. Finally he said, "My name is Jack and I am six years old. How old are you?"

Mike and I looked at each other quickly and then said, "We're six, too, and we're *still* going to walk on your wall." Little did we know from that day forward we would be the best of friends for the rest of our lives.

Pat. Mike. Jack.

Walls are meant to keep people out, but in this case, one particular stone wall formed a bond between three friends that would last a lifetime.

2

Today is Mine

"Friendship is the hardest thing in the world to explain. It's not something you learn in school. But if you haven't learned the meaning of friendship, you really haven't learned anything."

—*Muhammad Ali*

As we entered first grade, we were happy to see that our new friend Jack was also in our class; that was when we really knew we were the same age. We could continue to have fun together. It helped to soften the blow when summer ended.

I never liked school; perhaps it was because I thought my sister was smarter than I was, and somehow that just didn't sit well with me. The teachers would ask a question, and the minute Mike raised her hand to answer, I would too. The only difference was that I never knew the answer, but she always did! The teachers laughed at this, thinking it was all just a game we were putting on for their benefit, but I knew that despite our love for each other, we were in competition.

I guess you could say that the periods I liked the best were recess and lunch. I tried to be a good student, but it just didn't work for me. Some things came naturally; others didn't. For me, being a student just didn't come naturally. I sometimes felt that since we were twins, there was only so much of each thing to go around. In this case, I guess Mike got most of the smarts, and I got what was left over. My special talents hadn't yet emerged.

As for Jack, he usually knew the answers, but he never raised his hand. As it turned out, he couldn't have cared less. I always admired that about him; in fact, I wish I could have had that kind of confidence while growing up. I think that's why I was always drawn to him.

Through the years, and into our high school years, we would always be the three amigos: Pat, Mike, and Jack. We were always together during school hours. As if that wasn't enough, after school we'd go to each other's houses and hang out together. I'll never forget Jack coming over and sitting in my father's favorite chair. Dad would get so mad that he'd have to leave the room. It had to be more than just the chair. After all, we had plenty in our dream house. I think my father was jealous because he just didn't understand our relationship. I didn't see what was so hard to understand. We were best friends until the end.

There was nothing we wouldn't do for each other. You might be thinking "love triangle," and I'm sure that's what our classmates, neighbors, and other friends initially thought, but they were wrong. As we got older, Jack had his girlfriends, we had our boyfriends, and there was never any jealousy between us.

Still, we would always end up hanging out together, downtown or at each other's houses. Jack's mother always hoped he would marry one of us, but Jack was our best friend. With all that we went through—during elementary school, junior high, and high school—we never had any type of romantic relationship. Of course, that's not to say we didn't *think* about it from time to time, but I suppose it was just never meant to be. No matter how young or old we were, I think we all knew that crossing that line would ruin the friendship, and, in the end, the friendship was more important than the "might have been."

On the home front, my mother insisted on dressing us identically until we started the seventh grade. She would sew all of our clothes, including coats and suits, and eventually even prom dresses. This was in addition to her full-time job, her hobbies, and her other wifely and motherly duties.

My mom really worked harder than any other mother I knew about. In a vain attempt to follow her tireless work ethic, Mike and I both took piano lessons and dancing lessons (tap, jazz, and ballroom). We took swimming lessons at the local pond every summer, too. Despite all the skills and talents Mom had, swimming was something she had never learned how to do, but she was determined that we would.

We were popular little girls, and people loved to see us together. As such, Mike and I would tap dance together at every music recital: up and down steps one year, dancing to the musical hit "Me and My Shadow" the next. (Of course, I was the shadow.) We even won a dance contest when we were in the sixth grade and went on *Community Auditions,* a local TV show, only to be beaten out by a girl who recited the poem "In Flanders Field." What was *that* all about?

One day, our teacher asked my mother if we would perform for the students in our class. It was the same day as our recital. Since there was so much going on, my mother had rollers in our hair when we did our routine in front of the class that afternoon. (I guess you could call it a dress rehearsal.) We didn't think it was a big deal at the time, but looking back, I see what idiots we must have looked like. Idiots or not, the class liked it, and that was always enough for us.

Growing up, we spent most of our summer weekends at my aunt's house on a lake in Hopkinton. My cousin Lynn was four years younger than us. We would go up almost every weekend to water ski and hang out with Lynn. We were very close. Her mother and father were my godparents and I loved them dearly. Over the years, we would continue to grow up together, and remain very close.

Our best times, growing up, were on the lake. My uncle would take us for spins on the snowmobile and ice fishing. These are still some of my favorite memories. As the years passed, Lynn and I would go our own ways, but our love for one another remained. We would reunite thirty years later, and I would find that she was my inspiration of hope—an inspiration at a time when I thought I would never find myself again.

After eight years of piano and dance lessons, we both decided we had had enough. After all, we would be entering seventh grade at the junior/senior high school in the fall, and our number-one priority was going to be boys.

It was 1963, and change was in the air. We found out that we were going to be big sisters; my mother was pregnant, and our baby sister, Gloria, arrived on June 6. Mom may have been a hard worker, but she was a strategic planner as well. We were eleven at the time, which made us Gloria's official babysitters until she was old enough to go to school. (Talk about multitasking!)

And so we started our teen years together with our loyal friend Jack. The junior/senior high school was one school; from seventh grade until graduation, we stayed in the same school and knew everyone in our graduating class: All sixty-three of them.

3

The Teen Years

It was the best of times,
It was the worst of times;
It was the age of wisdom,
It was the age of foolishness;
We have nothing before us,
We have everything before us.

—Class of 1970

In the fall of 1963, we entered the seventh grade. Mike and I had grown taller, and, of course, we now wore bras. I was two inches taller than my sister, which made me feel a little awkward. Even though we weren't identical, I felt we should be at *least* the same height.

Apparently, I took after my father. He was tall, thin, and blond, with blue eyes. Mike took after my mother, who was short and thin with dark hair and brown eyes. Aside from our physical differences, Mike and I had very different personalities. My twin was more outgoing, while I was quiet and reserved. That would eventually change, but not for a long time.

Our first day in school was very intimidating. Being in the seventh grade set us apart from the older students, and despite the extra inches and padded bras, we felt very small and insignificant next to the upperclassmen. However, we did have one advantage. Our brother, Kenny, was a sophomore and just happened to be one of the most popular—and handsome—boys in school.

Kenny had brown eyes and blond hair. He was very athletic, and naturally all the girls wanted to date him. So, of course, when the girls in school found out that Kenny had twin sisters in junior high school, we suddenly had a lot of older "girlfriends." They might have been using us just to get to Kenny, but hey, it worked for us!

Our best friend, Jack, had an older brother that was Kenny's age, who just happened to be his best friend, so after those first few days of feeling awkward and small, we had it made. How could we lose?

Eventually we started enjoying all the attention, and we really took advantage of it. Our popularity wasn't the only sudden change, though; for the first time in our school years, we were separated during the day.

Since Mike was a better student, we weren't in any of the same classes. At long last, it was time to develop our individuality. Fortunately, our newfound popularity gave us the confidence to bridge this gap without too much disruption. Still, it felt odd to look to my left or right and not see Mike there. It definitely took some getting used to.

Fortunately, Jack was in some of her classes and in some of mine, so it still managed to work out well. Good old Jack: at least we always had him. Of course, being as handsome as he was, girls suddenly started getting *very* interested in him, which was not a plus for Mike and me. Jack was ours, he had been for seven years now, and no one was going to take him away from us *that* easily! That is, until *we* started getting boyfriends—then it was suddenly okay. (Funny how that worked out.) Still, no matter whom the three of us were dating, we still made time to spend a few hours every day with one another, usually after school. We were very close back then, but at the time we didn't know that Jack's friendship would become the most important part of our childhood, and, in fact, would continue forever. It would be under different circumstances, of course, but each of us knew we had a friend for life. It was a comforting thought through our turbulent adolescence.

As if school and friends and Jack and grades and boyfriends weren't enough, there was still our baby sister, Gloria, to deal with. Instead of sleeping late like the rest of my friends, I would wake up every Saturday morning when she woke up, take her downstairs, change her diapers, and feed her breakfast, so my mother could sleep.

Once Gloria got older, my sister and brother would tease and threaten her mercilessly, so it fell to me to be her unofficial protector. I would hide her in the closet, under the bed, or in the attic—anywhere they wouldn't find her.

My brother would say, "If I don't find you, I'll have to beat up Pat." Yes, it is true. I got the little beatings, because I told Gloria not to come out until I said so, no matter what.

One day, my brother found a pigeon with a broken wing in the backyard. He put it in a cage until its wing healed. When it did heal, I said, "Why don't you let the pigeon go? Its wing has healed."

Kenny said, "Because I don't want to, and if you let it go, you'll get a black eye."

Of course, being the tomboy that I was and being tough on top of that, I let the pigeon go. That afternoon, when my brother came home, he remained true to his word; I got my very first black eye. Naturally, Kenny told me not to tell my mother, so I didn't. She kind of guessed what had happened when she came home from work that night and saw that my eye was completely closed and already black and blue. Even though I wouldn't tell her who had done it, Kenny got a few bruises of his own! But the pigeon was free, and that was all that mattered to me.

Another time, my parents had a party with all of our aunts, uncles, and cousins. Naturally, we kids were all hanging out in my bedroom, playing games and talking, because we didn't want to hang out with the adults. Our bedroom was on the second floor, and there was a laundry chute that went down to the cellar, into which we would throw our dirty clothes.

Kenny and my cousin dared me to go down it, and without a care, I said, "Okay." I was hanging by my arms and ready to let go when my father came upstairs and yelled at me to climb out. Once again, Kenny was soundly punished.

Years later, we would all laugh about these things, but it must be true that God protects children and fools. In this case, my dad was the protector. He had saved me from two broken legs and lots of cuts, scrapes, and bruises that day. Eventually, my brother stopped daring me to do things, partly because he knew I would do them, no matter what, but mainly because he was just plain tired of being punished.

Dad wasn't the only hero in our house. My mother worked hard all week and also worked Friday nights. She worked as a teller in a bank and would eventually become the supervisor of the mortgage department. To say that she was tired by the end of the week is a bit of an understatement.

My mother would come home every day during her lunch hour and get supper started, and when my father came home from work at three-thirty, he would finish preparing the food and wait for her to get home to eat. You would think that with all of us kids, dinnertime would be a madhouse, but surprisingly, supper at our house was always quiet. My father would shut the TV off, and if the phone rang, we were not allowed to take the call.

My parents worked very hard, but like all married people, they had their own problems, which we only started to notice when we got older. My father was very smart, but despite his intelligence, he never had much confidence in himself. As a result, he tended to be very envious of my mother when she started getting all those promotions at work. They would fight a lot at night. It could get so bad that my sister and I would put pillows over our heads to block out the screaming and shouting.

My brother had come into his own by this time and was another reason for their fights. He was pretty wild, although he never got into anything too serious, and his grades were not what you'd call the best. Soon, he started becoming more upset about the fighting than we were, because he was older and could actually understand what was going on and could see the writing on the wall where our parents were concerned. What did Mike and I know about fighting? We thought that was what all parents did, but Kenny knew better, and over time, I could see it weighing down on him rather heavily.

Between the fighting and the underachieving, my big brother became very rebellious. He ended up being the brunt of my father's anger on many occasions. When he was a senior, he decided to quit school and join the Marines. Unfortunately, the Vietnam War was in progress, and we prayed that after he graduated from Paris Island he wouldn't be sent to Vietnam.

Our prayers were never answered. He was to fly over with his company two weeks after graduation.

4

Growing Pains

*"They thought the music would never die,
and the beat would go on forever..."*

—*Unknown*

As the days and years went by, Mike and I eventually went our separate ways, with different friends, different hobbies, and different views of the world. In spite of this divergence, or perhaps even because of it, my high-school years were the best years of my life.

Every day started out as good as the last, and then the next day would end up topping the one before that. We were insulated in our little community; I know that now. Perhaps it was because of all the fighting at home that I found school a safe haven, a refuge, and a relief.

There were dances, basketball games, and house parties, and when basketball season was over, there were baseball games, and when baseball season was over, there were football games. Weekends were meant for partying, going to the drive-in, and, now that my twin sister and I were finally fourteen, working.

Despite our differences, Mike and I both found jobs and worked in a rest home. I worked in the kitchen, delivering meals and washing dishes, while Mike worked as an aide to the nurses, feeding the patients, cleaning bedpans, and making sure the patients were comfortable.

Age hadn't dimmed our mom's inherited work ethic. We also babysat for the neighbors' children, which actually turned out to be kind of fun, because after the kids were tucked away in bed, we would have our friends or boyfriends over! Life was good.

By the middle of my freshman year in high school, I started dating a boy named Mark, who, as it turned out, would be my boyfriend for the next five years. My best friend Robin, also had a steady boyfriend, and together we would double-date all the time.

One night, we all went to the drive-in. Naturally, we had our boyfriends climb in the trunk, so we would only have to pay for two tickets. Once we were inside, Robin and I decided to take our time opening the trunk. We couldn't let them out until it got dark anyway, so we talked to them through the backseat, ate popcorn, drank soda, and generally just had a great time—that is, until it was finally time to let them out. The guys were not happy at all—not by a long shot. In fact, it was quite awhile before they would even talk to us, let alone be civil. Robin and I just laughed, and eventually, they both got over it. Robin and I always had a great time. We shared a lot of secrets, and we would remain close friends, thoughout the years.

My sister had decided that the guys in the next town were much better looking and older, so she and her friends would hang out in Milford on weekends, date different guys, party, and just have fun. Looking back, I think I missed out on the sense of freedom that she had, but I probably wouldn't change anything, even if I could.

Before we knew it, it was suddenly time for the junior prom. True to form, my mother made us beautiful prom dresses, then brought us to the hairdresser's, where we met some of our friends and talked about our dresses, dates, and the inevitable after-prom party.

At the time, my hair was long, reaching down to my waist and very straight. The hairdresser looked at my hair and didn't know how to curl it, so she washed it and put in giant rollers, and then put me under the dryer for a few hours. When she took the rollers out, my hair was straighter than it had been when I had arrived!

I left the salon, went home, and cried for the rest of the afternoon. My mother came to my bedroom and said, "Get dressed. I'll put a ribbon in your hair and you'll look beautiful." What she really meant was "plain is beautiful," of course, and she was right.

Off to the prom I went with a beautiful dress, a handsome boyfriend, and straight hair. When it came time to pick the prom queen, everyone was asked to come to the dance floor and dance so that the judge could make his selection. I remember telling Mike to come up with her date, but she couldn't have cared less. We all assembled and shook our groove things. The singer of the band watched us all dance, and then asked couples to leave until there were only seven couples left. He then came over and placed the tiara on my head, crowning *me* queen of the junior prom!

I couldn't believe it! It was one of the happiest days in my life. I remember thinking how amazed I was that my long, straight hair had won, over the beautiful curls in my court. Mark and I danced one dance alone, and then the six couples who made up the court joined in, followed by the rest of the class. What a night!

After the dance, we were to attend the after-prom party at my friend Paula's house. She lived a short distance from me, so I stopped by my house and told my parents I had been crowned queen of the junior prom. My mother said, "See? What did I tell you? Plain *is* beautiful." She was right once again.

Next I went in and woke up my brother, Kenny, so I could tell him the news. True to form, he said, "I don't believe you." (The stinker!) I immediately went to the kitchen, got my crown, and showed him. He just laughed, though, because he had really believed me all along, but once again had to play the big tease. That year, my boyfriend and I were also class marshals for the senior class, which was quite an honor, because the seniors voted on whom they wanted as their escorts for graduation from the junior class.

We started our senior year in the fall of 1969. Time went by quickly, and it was time to work on our yearbook: the dedication of the book, the "superlatives" of the class, pictures of students, sports teams, and so on. Our class voted on each "superlative." When the votes were counted, it turned out that I had been voted "Most Popular" of my class. But I wasn't alone in winning top honors from our small graduating class. Along with a fellow student named Neil, my twin sister, Mike, and our best friend, Jack, were voted "Most Flirtatious."

Finally, it was graduation day. We put on our caps and gowns, lined up with our partners—Jack by my side, and Mike behind me—and off we went down the hall, through the open doors of the auditorium, and up to the stage.

Along the way, I couldn't help but reflecting on the past, the present, and the future. For me, it was a day of happiness, but also a day of sadness. I was happy because I already knew what the world had showed me, and even though I didn't know what was ahead, I had a pretty good idea that if it was anything like life had been so far, I was in for a rollicking good time. But I felt sadness that I would be leaving my best friends to travel my own road. Still, it was tempered by the happiness I felt knowing that I'd had such a wonderful childhood, great friends, and memories that would last a lifetime. As I stood there waiting for my name to be called, I wondered what lay ahead. I would work through the summer for the telephone company, go to college in the fall, get married, have children, and live happily ever after.

But I would eventually learn that what you want is not usually what you get. I would learn that life had a far different plan for me. It would be a life that would test my choices, strength, and endurance over and over again.

I would become a stronger person for it and would go on to conquer life's ups and downs over and over again, until life's final test would send me to the darkest, deepest place I had ever known possible, a place I would not be able to—or want to—leave. And it was there that I would remain, and it was there that I would stay, because my soul finally would have lost the will to live.

5

An Act of Courage

"One sad thing about the world is that the acts that take the most out of you are usually the ones that other people will never know about."

—*Anne Tyler*

Two days after we graduated, Mike and I began our first official act as adults: we started working for the telephone company. Months earlier, a recruiter had come to our high school looking for seniors to recruit. She had explained, in detail, about the company, its benefits, vacations, health insurance, and paid holidays—the works. All we had to do was take a typing and math test, and if we passed, we could start work right away.

They weren't kidding. After graduating on June 5, we showed up bright and early for work on Monday, June 7, 1970.

Many of our good friends, including my double-dating friend, Robin, had also taken the test and passed. Jack had decided to become, in his words, a "professional student," so he enjoyed the summer, and then went to a junior college a few towns away. At least we still got to hang out on the weekends.

So off we went that first Monday morning to start our first real jobs with great pay and excellent benefits. I have to admit that it was a little overwhelming those first few weeks, what with not only learning our jobs, but also being out in the professional world as adults. So far the only adults we'd shared time with had been our teachers and our parents, but these were grown men and women: husbands, wives, mothers, and fathers; people with glasses and girdles and thinning hair and mortgages and car payments and insurance policies. They were not classmates or teammates; they did not share our memories, they had their own memories that, after all, didn't include *us*. However, we would be going to college in the fall so we made the best of it.

The seventies were the heady, hopeful days of the Carpenters, Barry Manilow, hip funk, and the Age of Aquarius; miniskirts, hot pants, halter tops, and motorcycles. The freedom to do just about everything was the battle cry of our hip, happening, with-it generation.

Naturally, it was a better-than-great time for me. I loved the freedom of riding a motorcycle. My steady boyfriend Mark had one all through our high-school years, so I was no stranger to the days of "Easy Rider," Jack Nicholson, and Peter Fonda. Even though Mom didn't like motorcycles because they were too dangerous, she trusted Mark enough to let me ride with him. The music, the fashion, the wind in my hair on the back of Mark's bike—what could be better than growing up in the seventies? Little did I know that 1970 would be the last year I would have of feeling that absolutely nothing in my world could be more perfect?

And thus the class of 1970 eagerly turned the page to the next chapter of our lives. On the pages of our personal histories, however, it turned out that our childhood friendships, despite our twelve years in school together, would not withstand the changes and decisions we all would have to make in our personal lives over that decade, and the others to follow. Our lives would cross often during the years to come, but we all would choose our own paths to follow. Some would be good, and some would be bad, but I knew that once I had chosen my path, it would be the only road for me—the road that would hold my future.

Mike and I grew up fast in the fast-paced professional world of the telephone company. We really had no choice. We realized that we had to in order to keep our jobs. My future sister-in-law Joanie worked in the same building, so she instantly became our friend and guide, and helped us through the first few weeks.

We met many wonderful people who, as the months went by, would become our new friends, replacing those we'd grown up with and from whom we'd thought we'd never part. The nervousness of that first timid Monday started to disappear as they helped us adjust to the working world. It was a time of endings and beginnings. Instead of clinging to the old friends who'd gone their separate ways, we started partying with our new friends on weekends and forming new friendships, some of which would last a lifetime. I would be remiss if I did not mention that we met so many great-looking engineers and technicians that summer of 1970 that it was hard to choose the ones we liked the best.

As fate would have it, Mike and I never made it to college after all. At the time, it just didn't seem to make sense. Who needed a piece of paper, we thought, to prove to us what we already knew? Besides, the money was great, and we had excellent benefits and a ton of new friends, and so we continued working for the telephone company. Mike left after a couple of years to marry and have children; I remained with the company for the next thirty-three years.

Suddenly, summer was behind us, and now it was the winter of 1970. Christmas was just a month away. With our own money, we bought Christmas presents for friends and family. Christmas was always a great holiday for us, not just because of the usual festivities, but also because our birthday was the day after Christmas. My mother and father would have a traditional Christmas like everyone else did, and the next night they would invite cousins and relatives over for our birthday. Mom always felt that since everyone else had separate birthday celebrations, so should we.

The family tradition, which had begun on our first birthday, involved my mother baking not one, but two birthday cakes, each in the shape of a Christmas tree. Next, she would cook dinner for everyone, and then Mike and I would kneel in front of the Christmas tree with our cakes, and candles would glow as everyone sang "Happy Birthday" to us. Then we would sit at the table and open our presents.

It was just like Mom not to combine our birthday with Christmas, thinking, "The heck with it; the kids will be so happy that they'll never know the difference." From that very first birthday, when we certainly wouldn't have known any better, she'd already foreseen the future and made it a point to separate what were the year's two biggest holidays, for us, anyway. So now, thanks to her, we always looked forward to this holiday the most. This Christmas would be different, though, for it would bring with it events so horrific for the whole family that it would take a piece out of our souls forever.

On December 11, 1970, Kenny went out with his friend for the evening. He had bought a car when he came back from Vietnam, flush with pay from the Marines. Armed with his freedom, off he went. Before he left on that fateful night, he said he would be home at around eleven. We had no reason not to believe him.

That night we watched television as usual, got our clothes ready for work the next day, and went to bed without a care in the world. For some reason—perhaps it was that very same uneasy feeling I would experience years later when I was a mother myself—my mother waited up for Kenny to come home.

She waited up all night, never going to sleep. I never knew how strong a mother's intuition could be until I experienced it myself. Mothers know when something isn't quite right; it's a feeling you can't describe. That was what my mother felt as December 11 dissolved into December 12, 1970.

The phone call every mother dreads came at 2:00 AM. My mother, still fully dressed as she was sitting rigidly during her all-night vigil, answered the call that would change her—and the rest of us—forever. After she hung up the phone on that still, quiet night, she woke up my father. While he was getting dressed, she came into our room and explained that Kenny had gotten into a car accident.

Though her blunt explanation made it sound so simple and clean, the truth was anything but simple or clean. Kenny's new car had hit a construction trailer and burst into flames. His friend had been thrown out of the car to safety, but Kenny had been trapped inside, and when he finally got the door open, he had started running. He had been in shock, and also on fire.

His friend had finally caught up with him and thrown him to the ground, using his coat to put out the flames. Kenny was immediately brought to the burn center at Massachusetts General Hospital, where they would eventually determine he had been burned over ninety percent of his body, with no chance of survival.

Despite his initial prognosis, he would end up staying there for the next five months, in and out of consciousness, struggling with pneumonia and infection after infection. When he was conscious, he would pray for death to release him from a pain so intense and unbearable that he did not have the will or the strength to live in this world anymore. So we waited for another dreadful phone call telling us that he hadn't survived. The call never came.

My mother and father drove to the hospital unit every day and stayed with him. They held his hand ever so lightly, afraid to cause him the intense pain that resulted from even the lightest of physical contact, but wanting to assure him that they were there.

Mercifully, he had been put on a morphine drip to ease the excruciating pain, and every day my parents waited patiently for any sign of recognition from their oldest child and only son, Kenny. The doctors had wrapped his entire body and face with bandages soaked in a saline solution. The only part of his body that wasn't covered was the area around his eyes.

Week after week, month after month, my parents drove to Boston every day. It was a two-hour drive there and back. To ease their parental duties, we took care of Gloria, the meals, the phone calls, and the house.

At long last, their grueling vigil was rewarded: Kenny was finally able to open his eyes and see them, but who knew where he went after that? People say there is a darkness, a place you go to when you're struggling to survive, a place that shields you temporarily from the world, from the pain, from life itself. Little did I know that I would end up in that same place years later, and, thanks to Kenny and his limitless pain on this earth, this is how I know where that darkness is and where he would stay for months to come.

My parents did not allow us to go in and see our brother, at least not for a while, anyway. They thought it would be too much for Kenny and also too upsetting for Mike and me. My mother and father had to return to work eventually, but my mother continued to go in every night after work and come home after we were in bed.

It was a long, cold New England winter, made doubly so by the bleakness in our frozen hearts. My father felt he should start spending more time at home, so he started staying home at night more often. It wasn't just for us: I don't think he could handle sitting next to the bed of a son who no longer recognized him day after day, night after night.

We welcomed having a father figure to send us off to bed each night, but we missed Mom being home. In general, it was a tough year for all of us. I remember my mother telling us once that even though she had four children that she loved equally, she would always be with the one that needed her most. There was no question which child that was this year, so we did our best to help out and to understand that she was where she needed to be.

We weren't the only ones concerned about Kenny. The telephone company where I worked held a blood drive and donated it all to my brother. It was the first time I truly realized what a great and compassionate company I worked for, and how not going away to college like many of our classmates, had been, for me, the right choice.

Eventually, Kenny started waking up a little more and recognizing his surroundings, and he eventually tried to talk to my parents. The doctors started operating, performing skin grafts with the skin that was left on that ten percent of his body that hadn't been burned. They would shave pieces of his skin a little at a time to graft onto the areas that had been burned. One of his ears had burned, and he no longer had eyelashes, but the worst surgery he had to endure was on his hands. Because the doctors had been convinced he was going to die, they had put his hands and fingers on a metal cast with his fingers bent. When the doctors realized he might just survive after all, they took off the cast. His fingers had been burned so badly that there was simply no choice but to cut off his fingers down to the knuckle and let the hands heal. One of his hands had been burned worse than the other. He needed a skin graft on the top of this hand. The doctors shaved pieces of his own skin from under his arm, grafted them to the hand, and wrapped his hand under his arm so the skin would grow. Just thinking about this made us upset. I can only imagine what Kenny must have felt, living through it.

By now it was almost Christmas. My father usually went out every year to get the Christmas tree and put it up. Then we would decorate the tree with ornaments that we had made in school over the years, bulbs, and lights. However, this year, Mike and I didn't want a tree. How could we celebrate Christmas, we thought, while Kenny lay in the hospital dying? Mom came home one night and we told her we didn't want a tree—or a birthday party—this year. My mother sat down; weary from working by day and driving to the hospital every night. She looked at us, and with all the strength she had left, said that she understood our feelings, but that she had three other children. We would have a Christmas tree and we would celebrate our eighteenth birthday.

Gloria was only seven, and even though Kenny was in the hospital, Mom would go ahead and celebrate the holidays with the rest of her family. My mother had become the rock of the family, with the courage, endurance, and undying inspiration that would help all of us get through the hard times and enjoy the good times throughout our lives. She would earn the respect of not only her family, but everyone that came into her life. She would never question God regarding why tragedies or bad times happened to her or her family, but instead would find the strength to get through it.

That year we received a special present from our parents: Mike and I were finally able to see Kenny on our birthday. It had been seven weeks, and we were anxious to visit for at least a few minutes. His girlfriend, Joanie, had been going in with my mother every night since the accident. Since we worked together, I would eventually take her in after work, and I found strength in her. I don't know if I could have gone through what she did.

She knew her life had changed forever. Her hopes and dreams of any future were put on hold until Kenny was better, but through it all, she never gave up. Joanie would continue for the next five months to go in, help change his bandages, help him walk, and offer him the courage to live again. That kind of love only comes once in a lifetime, and we thanked God for her, because we all realized that without my mother and Joanie, Kenny might have given up completely. If Joanie had any regrets along the way, no one ever knew about it. She won the ultimate respect from all of us for giving Kenny the will to live again. She became another sister to Mike, Gloria, and me. She was no martyr, just an angel sent from God who had given Kenny the ultimate gift of unconditional love.

As the weeks passed, Kenny started on the long road of recuperation. The doctors at Massachusetts General Hospital were amazed that he had survived this long. They put all his X-rays, daily charts, and taped surgeries in the Mass General book of people that had survived such severe burns after having been diagnosed as having no chance of survival.

So strong was his will to live, such an impact Joanie had made, and so advanced was his recovery that at long last, we were able to bring Kenny home for a few weekends in April and May. The timing couldn't have been better: Mike had become engaged and was to be married in May. We took Kenny home for the weekend so he could be there. It was a small wedding, with a reception held at home. Kenny was able to see our cousins and other relatives, who visited him in his room.

At the end of May 1971, he was finally released from the hospital for good. He came home with bandages over most of his body, and we were shown how to change his dressings, remove the dead skin with tweezers, and apply a saline solution to his open wounds.

Joanie and my mother did most of this; Mike and I would take care of him when needed. It was a long year for him. His recovery was slow and painful, but the rewards were, perhaps, more than he had expected: he was able to get married to Joanie in November 1971. They had a beautiful wedding, and eventually had two beautiful children. However, he would wear scars both inside and out for the rest of his life.

When I think back to what he was able to accomplish, I think my brother, Kenny, is the most courageous person I have ever known. His strength and will to live was an inspiration to everyone that knew him, and I learned how much respect and love I had for him—more than any other person I knew. And yes, in case you're wondering, I have long since forgiven him for the black eye and the bruises of my youth. I don't tell him that, of course. I continue to harass him about it whenever we are together, and he just continues to laugh. I suppose some things just never change.

Mark and I finally broke up, after a six-year relationship. What we once had shared, we both knew, had somehow evolved into something different. We had known each other so long and we had so many shared memories, we now felt more like brother and sister than boyfriend and girlfriend. One of the hardest things I ever had to do was to say good-bye to the boy, now a man, who had been my first love—The boy-man who had taught me how to drive, who had bought me beautiful jewelry, who had taught me how to ride a motorcycle and had treated me like a princess for six wonderful years. I will remember him always, with love and understanding, for what we had…and what we lost. We were destined to remain friends forever.

For a long time after that, it was hard for me to date. I was no longer in high school, where I had been sheltered from everything in the "real world." Back then I had known everything about everybody: where they lived, whom they'd dated before, where they sat in homeroom, who they'd taken to the prom. Now I didn't know whom to trust, so I trusted no one. Eventually, I grew up and tried to act my age—all of nineteen—and started dating a few guys.

I remember caring deeply for one man in particular. We worked together off and on for years. It was a different kind of relationship with a new man: safe and protective. For all our feelings, though, we never did anything, perhaps because he was older than I was. But he knew and I knew we felt the same way.

I think about him often now. I think about the wasted chances, the regret with hindsight, and the backward glances. Suddenly, it was too late for us. They say, "Time waits for no one." This relationship would prove no different. He remains forever in my heart, though, stored away in a place held for a chosen few. And over the next thirty years, as life would take away pieces from my soul, I would protect that small place and refuse to let life destroy it.

6

A Bend in the Road

Two roads diverged in a wood, and I—
I took the one less traveled by,
And that has made all the difference.

—Robert Frost

It was 1972, and my twin sister Mike was married, expecting her first baby, and living in Oklahoma with her husband Kevin, who was in the army. My brother Kenny and his new wife Joanie were expecting their first child. And me?

Well, I was still working at the telephone company. I had started dating a friend of my cousin's. Charlie was tall, with brown hair and blue eyes, and just so happened to be six years older than I was. Despite the minor age difference, it was love at first sight for me. I remember going to a club with my girlfriend. As soon as I got there, I saw my cousin Bernie at a table with some of his friends, so I went over and gave him a kiss and a hug, and he introduced me to Charlie and the rest of his friends. Two weeks later, Charlie called and asked me out. After that, we were inseparable. We were the ultimate seventies couple; together we would ride motorcycles, smoke grass, drink, go to clubs, and, in the immortal words of our favorite group, Van Halen, "dance the night away."

There were three couples we hung out with that had motorcycles around that time, and together, the eight of us had the best time of our lives. Charlie even tattooed my name on his arm, and my cousin painted my name on his helmet. We were together for almost two years, and lived together for a year and a half.

We would take the bikes up to New Hampshire and ride with other bikers and camp out in the woods, all the while having parties with friends and family. There just wasn't any room for anyone or anything else in my life but Charlie. I was so much in love with him that I couldn't imagine ever spending my life with anyone else.

We decided to get married in June 1974. One night shortly after our decision had been made, Charlie said, "Let's take a ride and see my mother." We were living two towns away, and I loved his family. So off we went to visit his mother and stepfather.

It was May 2, 1974. As we got on his Harley to leave, Charlie did a strange thing; I didn't think it strange then, but years later, I would. As we were about to leave, Charlie turned to his mother and stepfather and said, "I love you. I'll see you later." As we stopped at the end of the driveway, he turned his head and smiled at them and hesitated, as if, for the briefest of seconds, he didn't want to leave.

As we headed home, I thought, "What a beautiful night." And it was. It was warm, and the breeze felt wonderful. As we stopped at a stop sign, Charlie turned around, kissed me, and told me how much he loved me. Heading home, we turned onto Route 16, which was a main road in Mendon. It was around seven-thirty at night, and as we started down the road, a car was approaching from the opposite direction.

Then, just as we started to pass the driveway of a restaurant, the car just turned, without signaling. I remember Charlie telling me to hold on as I heard the screech of his protesting tires. In an instant I found myself flying over the motorcycle and landing on my stomach some twenty-five feet away. Then there was nothing No sound, just the awful silence that always precedes tragedy.

I remember thinking I was dead because I had no feeling in my body. After a toss like that, I should have been crying, screaming, and squirming with pain. But now I was somewhere quiet and peaceful. It was a place I didn't want to come back from, because I knew that once I got back, I would never be the same again.

I tried to lift my head up, but my helmet felt so heavy that I just gave up. I tried calling for Charlie, but he never answered me. I tried to drag myself across the gravel to look for him, but my body felt so heavy that I simply couldn't move. I couldn't focus my eyes. Then panic set in, as my whole body became numb. I didn't know where I was; I might have been in the road, on the grass, or in the parking lot of the restaurant. I didn't know who was with me. I drifted in and out of consciousness, dazed and confused.

In my dazed state, I felt the warmth of my own blood dripping down my face. My hands were covered with blood. I thought to myself, "My nails are broken"—a stupid thought at the time, I know, but such are the random firings of your brain when shock starts to set in. Then, out of nowhere, I heard a strange, raw-edged sort of scream, over and over again, until I finally realized it was coming from me.

And as I lay looking up at the sky, I saw Charlie, looking down at me with his beautiful blue eyes. I tried to get up, and he turned his head and smiled, then he was gone. I never knew whether I imagined this heavenly vision or actually saw him leave this earth, but it was then that I knew my life would never be the same. A piece of my soul had left my body with Charlie.

It seemed like forever before I felt someone touch me and ask me if I was okay. I looked toward this person without lifting my head and said three simple words: "Where is Charlie?"

She looked at me with great anguish, took my hand, and said, "Just stay still. The ambulance is on its way." Once again I slipped back into unconsciousness, afraid to wake up and hear those final words, the words that would haunt me the rest of my life. It turned out that the woman was a waitress who had come out of the restaurant when she heard the accident. She stayed with me and even came to the hospital in the ambulance in order to comfort me each time I woke up. She was a stranger, holding my hand as I looked at her with pain and fear in my eyes. Her sympathy and concern stayed with me for a long time because she made a difference in the life of someone she didn't even know. Suddenly, there were people everywhere trying to see the victims of the accident. The police were trying to keep the growing crowd away from the scene, while directing traffic from both sides. Through the hazy fog of semi consciousness, I could hear the sound of an ambulance in the distance. As I lay there, I tried to understand what was happening. I wasn't supposed to be here. It was all just a bad dream, and I would wake up soon and see Charlie lying beside me at home. We were safe in bed, with another lazy morning stretching out before us. There was simply no other explanation.

Then it was right back to reality. Suddenly, two EMTs were at my side. One was asking me my name and trying to get my vital signs while putting a neck brace around my neck; the other one was putting a leg brace on my leg. I just stared at them helplessly, hoping in vain that they would stop and simply leave me alone. Although they were being as gentle as possible, the pain from my contorted limbs was excruciating.

Once I was placed on the stretcher and safely inside the ambulance, I looked for my unknown friend. Was she really an angel in disguise? I must have passed out again, because I didn't see her right away. When I came to, however, she was right there, and had been there all along, I would later learn, still holding my hand. It was, thankfully, a short ride to the hospital. I was brought into the emergency room, where the doctors treated me for a concussion, stitched my wrist, and tried to clean the cuts and bruises as best they could.

Apparently, when I had been thrown from the motorcycle, I had landed on the street, and there were tiny stones and dirt embedded in the cuts. It turned out that I didn't have a broken leg after all, but instead had suffered a severe hematoma on my thigh, so I wasn't able to walk. The medical attendants brought me to a room for the night for observation.

As I lay there in the dark, doped up on pain medication but still feeling the occasional tidal wave of massive aches and pain, my brother walked in. He looked at me with concern, and something else that I couldn't quite understand. He said he had talked to the doctors and asked to have me released so he could bring me home. After much hesitation, they had agreed, but only if I was brought home and put straight to bed, and someone would have to be there to watch me at all times, in case of internal bleeding. I was under strict doctor's orders not to get up or walk for several days.

So I went home. As I sat in Kenny's car during the short drive home from the hospital, he avoided my eyes. I didn't ask the question that was hanging there like a noose in the dead air, because I knew he wouldn't be able to tell me—not yet.

I got home to find my parents, my sisters, and some of my relatives there. I hobbled on my new crutches over to the couch and lay there, waiting anxiously to ask the question that I somehow already knew the answer to, but I stopped myself. I guess I just did not want to hear the final answer.

My cousin and some of my friends eventually showed up. They were very concerned about me, but were all still silent about the unanswered question that hung in the air. Finally, my father came in. I couldn't take it anymore. It seemed to me that if it was good news, which I seriously doubted, it would be better to know it sooner rather than later. If it were bad news, it would be better to get it over with. After an awkward silence, I asked, "Where is Charlie?"

He stared at me for a few minutes before finally saying, "Do you think you can handle the answer?" I nodded, and as I started crying, he told me Charlie had been killed instantly upon impact. As I put my head back on the couch in shock, I suddenly realized why the doctors had let me come home; my family wanted to be the ones to tell me. They had been afraid I would hear it in the hospital the next day.

As I cried, I thought that maybe I had really seen him leaving this earth, after all; maybe it wasn't a dream, and he had really been saying good-bye as his last act on this earth. I cried for the marriage that would never be, for the happiness I would never feel again, and also for the lost innocence of that seventeen-year-old girl so many years ago. Yes, I would go on to recover, but I would never be the same again. I was destined to go through life afraid to show my true feelings, afraid to trust, afraid to let down my walls, always thinking that I would lose everyone that I loved.

My fear would eventually become a reality, and I would later find out that the man who had hit us had actually gotten out of his car and walked into the bar to order himself a drink, never once looking at us or at what he had done.

The wake was held two days later. My family attended, and my cousin Lynn wrote a letter from me to Charlie and left the letter with a red rose in the coffin. It read: *Charlie, I love you with all my heart forever and always, now until eternity. Pat.*

Unfortunately, I was physically unable to attend, because of my grave injuries. I had cuts and bruises over my entire body. Black and blue masses, that were sore to the touch and made sitting, lying, turning, or walking sheer agony, covered me, including the bottoms of my feet!

I was severely depressed and in a state of denial about the entire incident. On the morning of the funeral, I woke up and my twin sister, Mike, was sitting by my bed. I asked her what day it was, and when she told me, I suddenly realized that my parents had gone to the funeral without me, not wanting—or not daring—to wake me up. I suppose I understood; parents always try to protect their children from hurt and pain. I found the strength to get up because I felt that I truly needed to be there. Not going to the wake had been devastating enough for me, and now I felt that I needed to say good-bye.

Thank God Mike was there for me that fateful day. She immediately got a black dress out for me, helped me into it, and drove me to the church. By the time we got there, the funeral procession was already at the cemetery. My sister pulled up to the cemetery, parked, and helped me out of the car. Even on crutches, I could still barely walk.

When we arrived, the priest was talking, so I stayed back and waited for him to give the final blessing before approaching the gravesite. By now my family had come over and was standing with me. My friends were there, and so was my cousin Lynn, with a flower in her hand. I soon realized why; she gave me a red rose to put on the casket.

When the priest finished his prayers, Charlie's family came over and hugged me as we all cried. I waited for everyone else to leave, and then, with the help of my family, I went over and placed the single red rose from Lynn onto the casket.

As I stood there with the morning sun shining through the clouds, I looked around at the headstones of others who had passed away before Charlie, and, suddenly I felt a slight breeze move through my hair, ever so lightly. I stood there with tears running down my face. I cried not only for myself and for a life cut so tragically short, but also for Charlie's family, and I prayed that God would help ease their pain and suffering in the trying months to come. I had lost a fiancé, but they had lost a son. Even in my deepest grief, I knew I couldn't imagine how they must have felt.

Standing there at Charlie's final resting place was maddening. Even though I'd naturally expected to be sad, I had not known how hard it would be to say goodbye, yet it was harder still when I refused to say it.

How do you prepare yourself for such a tragedy? How do you go on with your life, knowing you'll never be the same again? How do you wake up the next morning, knowing you'll never see your best friend again? How do you cope with the knowledge that life is so short? You are forced to live every day as if it were your last, And you wonder where you'll ever get the strength to survive and move on. I would learn the answers to these questions years later, when life would once again send me to a gravesite, allowing me to finally answer those questions, once and for all.

But first, justice had to be served.

As the days turned into weeks, I slowly healed, physically, at least. I had moved back to my parents' house, and my mother had taken some time off of work to take care of me. It was more than just moral support; I couldn't walk because of the blood clot in my thigh. The doctors were still watching it very closely, monitoring its size and making sure it didn't get any bigger, or, worse yet, go anywhere. Meanwhile, I couldn't use the crutches very well, because I had split my wrist open, and once the stitches were removed, I had to let that heal. I was about as far from self-sufficient as one could get.

It often felt like no time had passed at all. The only way I could tell that I was slowly healing was from the outside: the cuts and bruises over my entire body went from an ugly and painful green and yellow to an ugly and painful black and blue. The bottoms of my feet were still cut and bruised, so my mother would have to help me into the shower, wash my hair, and cook for me.

On the professional front, I would be out of work for at least two or three months while I fully recovered. Thankfully, the telephone company, had taken up a collection for me just after the crash and sent flowers and cards, continued to be understanding, assuring me that my job would be waiting for me when I was back on my feet.

Thus assured, I'd lie on the couch day after day and let my body heal. Mentally, I don't know where I went. I refused to believe—on a conscious level—what had happened, and waited for some kind of miracle to bring my lover back to me. It never came. What did come, however, was a summons to appear in Milford District Court to testify against the man who had hit us. I was the only witness, and the court date was scheduled for June 4, 1974, a full month after the accident. By that time, my cuts and bruises had healed to the point where I could at least make the trip, and though I was far from back to normal, I was feeling more hopeful that I would at least get there someday.

As I hobbled up the stairs to the courthouse on my crutches with my family by my side, I thought to myself, "Finally, justice will prevail." As I sat on the bench in the courtroom, I watched and waited for the man who had been accused of vehicular manslaughter to walk in. Funny, here was a man who had taken everything that ever meant anything to me, and I didn't even know what he looked like until he was pointed out to me.

He happened to be the brother of the judge in Milford. This meant that another judge would hear the case and decide if there was probable cause for further hearings. As I was helped up and brought to the witness stand to testify against this stranger, I knew this man would go to jail for a long time. Not only had he been drinking and driving that fateful afternoon, but he had killed someone. Wasn't that enough to convict a man, even if his brother was a judge?

After I gave my testimony, which was a heart-wrenching experience, too painful to recall word for word, I was helped down from the witness stand back to where I had been sitting. I didn't notice the eyes of the courtroom upon me, or the hushed whispers of those who most surely thought, "How does she do it?" As for me, it was as if a great weight had been lifted from my shoulders, and as I sat there, the courtroom whirling around me, I felt like I had finally avenged Charlie.

The guilt over being the only survivor of our accident finally disappeared. Now, as we all waited for the judge to decide this obviously guilty man's fate, I looked over to see the man himself and noticed how his eyes remained fixed somewhere straight ahead. He never turned to look at me—not once. I realized that he hadn't even looked at me while I'd been on the witness stand.

In the end, the judge found him innocent of any wrongdoing. There was no loss of his license, no slap on the wrist, nothing. As the judge's mouth moved and his words leaked like poison out into the courtroom, I simply could not believe what I was hearing. My family told me later that it looked as if I was visibly deflated. I have no doubt of it, as that's exactly how I felt: empty, betrayed, broken, and defeated. Moments earlier I had been hopeful that this man would be off the streets, perhaps for good. Now I was sure he would be driving home that very day. It had taken so much out of me to get up on that witness stand and relive the memory so vividly, with such recall that thirty years later; the memories would still be there.

In the wake of the judge's verdict, I had a vivid flashback; for a few seconds, I was back on that motorcycle. Running everything through my mind in slow motion, I knew that what I had seen and what I had said on the stand was accurate. This man had literally gotten away with murder!

"Of course," rationalized the legal eagles, "being the brother of a judge did not affect the decision." Yeah, *right*. Did they think we believed that? I was helped up to leave, while he just sat there smugly in his triumph. As I walked by him, I lost control and screamed, "You killed my boyfriend and got away with murder!" I actually tried to hit him with my crutch, and almost fell! As I stood there, trembling with unanswered vengeance, he just shook his head and looked away.

That was my first encounter (although not my last) with a justice system that, despite all the evidence, let a guilty man go free. He was not punished for drinking and driving and not punished for taking the life of a thirty-year-old man who was so much more than just another statistic. Charlie had been my lover, my fiancé, my best friend, my partner, my mate, and an all-around good guy; and he deserved better.

I knew from that moment on that any illusions I'd had about the American justice system working were forever destroyed. The future was gone, and all that mattered to me was today—this moment—right now. Never again would I plan ahead, because after all I'd been through, I would never know if I would be there to enjoy it. And so I healed on the outside, but my heart had been broken. At the tender age of twenty-one, I had already seen and felt enough tradgey to last me a lifetime. I had lost all reason and predictability. I had lost all sense of comfort and security. I had lost all hope for the future. In the process, I had lost my own self. And I would continue my journey on the road to destruction, a journey filled with pain and revelation, awakening and changes.

7

Sunrise

"Today, a new sun rises for me; everything is animated, everything seems to speak to me of my passion, everything invites me to cherish it."

—Anne de Lenclos

As the days and months went by, I often had nightmares about Charlie and the accident. They seemed so real to me and so vivid, yet I pretended to myself that it had never even happened. I wanted to forget and move on, yet for some reason, I simply couldn't. It was then that my mother started calling me her "wild child."

I would look in the mirror and see a stranger staring back at me: someone who looked older than she was, who wasn't sleeping well, and whose hooded eyes masked a profound sadness. It was as though I were looking at someone else. By the fall of that year, I was beginning to move on. I finally went back to work. I was still on crutches, and though I had healed physically, emotionally it was a whole different story.

I held all my feelings in and never talked about the accident—or Charlie. I didn't talk about these subjects until years later. I would go the cemetery and sit there by myself, no matter what the weather was like or what time of day it was, and ask why this had happened. I never got any answers or felt that he was there with me, like others claim to do. I felt entirely alone and bereft. I'd always lived my life with purpose and passion; now it was hard to get out of bed, and once my feet were on the ground, to make them move and take me to the places I needed to go.

Eventually, I started going out with friends, started drinking again, and tried to heal my soul by keeping busy and crafting a "normal life" for myself. I started dating again, and eventually married.

I knew from the beginning that it was a mistake, just as I also knew the walls, locked doors, and prisons of my mind and heart were the ones I had built for my own survival. Even as I accepted his proposal, I knew I would never feel the way with him that I had with Charlie. But then, I knew that I would never feel that way again with anyone, ever, so I took the plunge and said, "I do."

From the first year on, I was so different that I hardly knew myself, and, truth be told, I really didn't care. By the time I was twenty-four, I found out I was pregnant. When the nurse called and said my test had been positive, I sat down and tried to be happy. I had no feelings. I hadn't been trying to get pregnant, but here I was, three months along, with a baby due in May.

The weird part was that I wasn't alone. Amazingly, my twin sister Mike was also pregnant with her second child. My new husband and I bought a house five minutes from Mike and her growing family and together we all waited anxiously for the babies to be born.

On May 28, 1977, after six hours of labor and without medication, I gave birth to a beautiful five-pound, twelve-ounce baby boy. I named him Louis. He was so tiny. I couldn't believe he was mine. He had the finest blond hair and big blue eyes, and when I held him I felt something I had never felt before: a love so strong and so powerful that I never wanted to let him go.

When the nurse put him in the nursery and brought me back to my room, I lay there waiting for the feeling to leave me. It never did. It was the strangest emotion: a feeling of two people existing only for each other. I knew it would be the truest, strongest, most honest feeling I would ever have. I also knew that my husband, the baby's father, wasn't included in the trio, because this love was only big enough for the two of us to share.

The next morning, Louis was brought in to me just as the sun was rising. As he lay in my arms with his eyes wide open, it seemed as though we were both looking toward the sun as it rose over the horizon, pushing away the morning darkness and opening up all the colors of the rainbow. Even then, I knew it wasn't just another day. Through all the hurt and pain, through all the tragedy and drama, there was one thing life had not stolen from me: redemption—a chance to do it over again. Now that I had taken that chance, nothing and no one would ever stop me from feeling this way again.

I was sent home from the hospital the next day, and from then on, Louis was the love of my life. I had always thought that saying was only for a spouse or a boyfriend, but to me it was for Louis. I had built up a wall in my heart that would not allow me to love another again as I had loved Charlie. I was always afraid that I would lose someone else I loved.

Now I made up for lost time and gave every inch of love I had left to Louis. Little did I know that he would be my whole world for the next twenty-one years. Through twenty-one years of trials and tribulations, of good times and bad, we shared a love that would test every piece of me, but a love so strong that even in death, it would never be diminished.

I had taken a six-month leave of absence from work to spend with my baby. When I brought him home from the hospital he was so tiny that much of him fit in the palm of my hand, with his legs just barely touching my elbow. His stomach was so small that he could only drink four ounces of milk at a time. For the first two months of his life, Louis was up every two hours. By the end of the second month, my pediatrician said to give him a teaspoon of cereal before he went to bed to see if it would help him sleep a little longer. I was so tired from getting up with him and tromping back and forth from the nursery that I had put the bassinet next to me in my bedroom so I would always hear him when he woke up. With the doctor's advice fresh in my mind, I fed Louis a little cereal before bed one night.

Amazingly, I slept like a baby and woke up at seven o'clock the next morning. When I opened my eyes, I saw the sun shinning through the curtains, and I realized it was morning. All of a sudden, I realized that Louis had not awakened during the night. I looked in the bassinet and saw that he was sound asleep. We had finally been able to get seven hours of uninterrupted sleep.

Over the next three months, I moved seamlessly into motherhood and forgot all about the business world. For the first time in my life, I was able to love my son and enjoy my life because nothing else mattered, not even my wounded soul. Louis seemed to erase all those old feelings of loneliness and hurt, and I pushed them yet deeper and deeper into my soul, so I would never have to face them again.

Every morning when I got up, I would watch him sleeping, and I could never imagine loving him more than I did at that very moment. As he grew older, I found I could love him even more. Louis grew very slowly, which had surprising side effects: he was crawling at five months and walking at ten months.

We had so much fun together. I never wanted to go back to work. We played all day. I bought an infant seat for my bicycle, strapped him on the back, and would ride for miles and miles. He would put his head back and laugh and laugh because he loved the feeling.

That was a beautiful summer, in more ways than one. But, like they say, all good things must come to an end. After three months of staying home with Louis, I realized that I would have to go back to work sooner than I had thought, because I needed the money.

On August 10, 1977, which just happened to be my brother Kenny's birthday, I went to my workplace with Louis and signed papers stating I would return earlier than my initial leave had specified. On the way home, we stopped at my mother's house, because she was having a special dinner and a birthday cake for Kenny. After the cake was served, I left and went straight home.

During the night I started getting sharp stomach pains and developed a fever, and I ended up throwing up the entire night. Despite the severity of my condition, I didn't want to go to the hospital because I thought I just had the flu. By morning it was worse, so off to the hospital I went. During the ride, I swore ruefully that Kenny had been up to his old tricks and put something in my food.

The doctors disagreed; they examined me, and, baffled, decided to admit me for more testing. They eventually found that my appendix had burst, so off to surgery I went, cursing my brother every inch of the way to the operating room. Of course, he never was the cause of this event (or so he said for years afterward whenever I brought it up), and the doctors told me it was common after having a baby. I stayed in the hospital for two weeks, while my family watched Louis and brought him in to see me every day.

Once I was released from the hospital, I went home to heal and spent the next three months with Louis. As my strength returned, I realized that Louis was getting bigger and more fun to play with. I would read him stories, and as my stomach healed more and more each day, I would dance with him in my arms to Barry Manilow's pop hits, "Can't Smile without You" and "Daybreak." As I turned and whirled while we danced, Louis would put his head back and just laugh, much like he had during our daily bike rides that blissful first summer of his life. It was such a beautiful time in our lives.

He would follow me as if he were my shadow. I would turn around, and there he would be, right behind me. I would go into the bathroom, and when I came out, there he was waiting for me. Talk about no privacy!

Summer turned into fall, as it must, and I prepared to go back to work in November. I had found a day-care center that seemed to have a great reputation and was only a mile from my house. I dreaded the day I would have to take Louis, drop him off, and leave him there for the day, but I had no other choice. To prepare for the inevitable, I spent as much time with Louis as I could that

October, bringing him to his regular doctor's appointments, going to the park, and riding my bike with him strapped onto the back.

Around this time, my manager at work called to ask me if I was interested in a supervisor's position. I had been a clerk for seven years, and instinctively I knew that a management job would mean more money. So I said yes and waited for her to call back sometime during the week, after they had completed interviews with the other candidates.

The call came three days before I returned to work; I had gotten the job and would be supervising twenty-five clerks, all of whom I had been working with before I left to have Louis. It was bittersweet news. I was thrilled at the new earning potential, but I already had so much change in my life as it was. Could I handle another change?

As I had expected, my first day back at work was a nightmare. Gone were the lazy days of summer. Now I had to get into a routine of taking a shower and getting myself ready for work before waking up Louis.

As one might expect, he was not very happy about getting up at seven o'clock in the morning. As I got him dressed and fed him, my heart was breaking the whole time, knowing what he did not: that soon we would be apart for the whole day.

When I brought him to the day-care center, I kissed him, held him tight, and told him how much I loved him. I put him down, and he started crying and putting his arms out for me. My heart was breaking in a thousand pieces as I left and got in my car. I cried all the way to work.

But once I pulled into the parking lot, there was no time for tears. I was starting my new job that day. Instead of resenting my promotion, my friends were happy that I would be their supervisor. Fortunately for me, they were great workers, and we all developed a friendship I will never forget. I would hear from them twenty years later, when we had all gone our different ways, moving on to other jobs, retirements, and promotions, but united by a bond that would bring us back to the old days again.

After that first auspicious day of getting back to work, life went on. I worked, took care of Louis, and started working out at the gym. Physical fitness had always been important to me, and now that I had recovered from the accident and the birth of Louis, I was even more passionate about my regimen. Gone were the old days when I was footloose and fancy-free, now I worked out on my lunch hour so that when I got home from work at five-thirty and picked up Louis, I would be able to spend time with him.

As all working mothers do, I felt I had to make up for the eight hours I was away from him in the few hours I had left at night. After trying in vain to keep my marriage together for the sake of my son, I filed for divorce when Louis was two, and far from regretting it, I was relieved that now our lives were finally the way they should have been: Lou and I against the world as we reached for everything that would bring us happiness.

We would protect each other against all the pain and sorrow in the world, and I was determined that we would have the richest lives possible. It was a beautiful dream, but a dream that would end so tragically that it would destroy me, until the fateful day that Louis would return and show me how to move on. Only then would I finally believe that we had the strongest love, not only in life, but also in death.

8

A Little Piece of Heaven

"A mother's love for her child is like nothing else in the world. It knows no law, no pity, it dares all things, and crushes down remorselessly all that stands in its path."

—*Agatha Christie*

Louis and I tried to make a celebration of each and every day, but the best times we had together as mother and son were going down to the Cape every summer. We made it an annual event, and far away from the pressures of work and home, we limited ourselves to doing nothing but playing, swimming in the ocean, and catching crabs.

My parents had always brought us to the Cape during the summer when we were growing up, and it made me proud to be able to recreate the tradition with my own child. I remembered how my mother and I would sit for hours just soaking in the sun, digging for quahogs, and finding the perfect shells. So I continued the tradition with Louis. I would rent a cottage every summer on the Cape, and we would go either alone, or with family or friends. I made a promise to myself that we would do this for as long as I could afford it, no matter what. It wasn't always easy, but looking back, I know that it was well worth it.

Louis loved the ocean, as I did. Once he was on the beach, he would start making sand castles right away. I would take him swimming, and as he got older, he would swim for hours with his friends or cousins. Of all our favorite memories, our vacations at the Cape were the very best.

There is something about the ocean that seems to take all your troubles away. I always found inner peace while sitting there on the beach, watching the waves rolling onto the shore in an endless series of fizzing sea foam. I think that because we can never see the end and never get past the horizon, time seems to stop and we forget all our problems and savor every minute we are there.

As the sun would start to set and people would slowly disappear, I would take Louis's hand and we would set off, just the two of us, and run along the shore, climbing rocks, collecting shells, looking for crabs, and doing whatever else struck our fancy. As we ran on the sand, I would pick him up, swing him around, and then hug him close to me, never wanting to let him go. I never wanted the happiness to disappear from his sunburned little face. I would remember it years later, and that memory would keep me alive, even when I wanted to die.

It was the closest we ever were to each other, and a bond of love, trust, and protection was formed between the two of us, glued together by those carefree summers on the shore—a bond that would touch our souls and stay there forever. No matter what happened over the years, we would always have a place together that was safe and free from any hurt and pain. I called it our little piece of heaven. It was at those times that I knew my life would never be my own again Louis would grow up and I would have to let him go, but we would keep these memories forever.

He was almost three years old now and was so beautiful with his blond curly hair and big blue eyes that were almost too big for his tiny face. He was so darling, in fact, that it was hard to get mad at him.

I remember waking up in the middle of the night with a banana peel on my face. Apparently Louis had crawled out of his crib, gone downstairs with his favorite yellow blanket, eaten a banana, came back upstairs, and put the banana peel on my face. The first thing I heard in the dark of night was Louis laughing because he had scared me. One look at him, with his one-piece Mickey Mouse pajamas and I started laughing so hard neither one of us could stop. In the end, he crawled into my bed with his yellow blanket and fell asleep.

At night when I put him to bed, I would snuggle up to him, tell him I loved him, and go downstairs. We started a little bedtime game. As soon as I started going down the stairs, he would scream, "I love you, Mom!" and I would pretend to fall all the way down the stairs. He would laugh and keep saying it, like we had a million stairs. I often wondered if he really wanted me to fall, because this lasted for years. Maybe that rascal Kenny had told him to do this!

One morning when he woke up, he came into my room, his favorite yellow blanket trailing behind him as usual, and climbed into bed with me. As we watched cartoons, I looked at him, so warm, happy, and content. I said, "I love you."

Louis said, "I love you too."

Not content with that answer, I asked him how much he loved me. With the most sincere expression on his face, he said, "Way past Jesus." Where he had come up with that, I never knew. I did know, however, that it was as much love as anyone could give. In later years, we would joke about it, but he continued to say this until his final days.

Despite our almost blissful happiness, however, a few things bothered me during those first five years of my son's life. From the time he was an infant, Louis would wake up screaming, and every time I would go in to find out what was wrong, he would wake up and never remember if he had had a nightmare or had just been scared of something. Amazingly, this lasted until he was in his early teens. When he had nightmares, I would bring him into my room with his favorite stuffed animal and yellow blanket, and he would fall fast asleep. As he got older, however, the nightmares continued, so I put his sleeping bag under my bed. On those nights, he would come in my room, pull the sleeping bag out himself, and fall asleep holding my hand.

Another thing that concerned me was a birthmark on the side of his nose that had developed over the first two years. I got so tired of people asking both of us what had happened to his nose that I taught him to say to anyone asking, "It's a beauty mark, and it makes me handsome."

They would just stare and agree. "Why, yes, you are one handsome little boy."

He also had stomach problems. When I took him to the doctors, they would say nothing was wrong. It always bothered me, though, and instinctively I knew it was more serious than that. Then one night he woke up and said his stomach "was sick." This started happening when he was around four years old. I would go in, make sure he wasn't sick, and put my hand on his stomach. I would tell him to shut his eyes, and I would hum for a few minutes, and all of a sudden, he would open his eyes and say his stomachache was gone. Now, I knew I had done nothing, but he must have thought I had some kind of special power, so whenever he had a stomachache, that was how I made it go away. It always amazes me how vulnerable and trusting children can be.

Life went on. I taught him how to ride a bicycle with the training wheels on, and soon he was riding without them. I brought him to swimming lessons, and by the time he was five years old, he was swimming like a fish.

In those days, I had two passions: Louis and work, in that order. As I learned about my second passion, the management world—managing people, treating them like I would want to be treated, managing a budget, improving my supervisory skills—I began to have problems with Louis's day care.

He was three years old, and so far he had been kicked out—or, as they so delicately put it, "You will have to find another day-care center for your son"—of not one, but two day-care centers. How does a three-year-old child get kicked out of day care? He was acting out and just plain angry. Of course, I blamed myself for having to go back to work, so I tried to spend even more time with him, devoting all my extra time during the week and on weekends to giving him all my attention. I would sit on the couch and read to him every night, play games with him, and try to teach him not to be so quick to get angry with other children.

Once again, I had to find another babysitter. Charlie's sister was babysitting for other children, so I called and asked if she had one more opening, and, of course, she made room for Louis. I was so glad to leave him every morning with someone I knew would be great with my son—someone I trusted.

Even so, the first morning was, once again, just plain awful. Although I could trust Charlie's sister implicitly, as far as Louis was concerned, I was leaving him with someone he didn't know. As I started to leave, he ran over to me and grabbed my leg, crying and saying, "Don't leave me, Mommy, I'll be good. I promise."

And once again the tears in my eyes started to overflow. I bent down to Louis and said, "This has nothing to do with you being bad. Mommy has to work. You'll love your new babysitter, and I'll bring you home a surprise tonight."

Louis stopped crying and said, "Promise?"

Relieved, I said, "Yes, I promise." When I picked him up that night, I had a small orange plush tiger behind my back. When he saw it, he cuddled it close and said, "I'm going to name him 'Prize.'" With that came my decision that, for the rest of my life, anytime I made a promise to Louis, I never would break it. No matter what else happened to him while he was growing up and going through life with all of its inherent pain and sorrow, at least he would know that once I made a promise to him, it would never be broken. He would have no doubts about that. And yet I did break a promise—just once, but once was all that mattered.

My divorce became final when Louis was almost four. After that, I had a year to sell my house, at the court's request. At the end of that year, we moved to Westboro, Massachusetts, and lived in a condominium. It was a two-bedroom unit with a pool for the whole development. As you drove into the area, there was a huge sign surrounded by beautiful flowers that the association kept up from early spring until late fall. I always looked forward to seeing those flowers on my way home each night.

Louis would start kindergarten in the fall, but once again, I had to find someone to watch him for half a day while I was at work. After checking out local daycare centers, I found one close to the school. A bus would pick him up for school and drop him off at day care in the afternoon. Of course, he was no angel there, either, and I was glad when the year ended and he would finally be attending first grade. To close the gap between the end of school and the end of my workday, after the bus dropped him off, my neighbor would watch him for a few hours until I got home from work.

I had dated a few guys since my divorce, but none seriously. Frankly, I had more fun with my girlfriends, because it was the first time I had time to spend with "just us girls." We went to clubs and parties, we went shopping, and did whatever we felt like doing, and it was great not having to answer to anyone. At long last, I got to choose who I wanted to date and who I didn't.

For three years, I led the life of a single girl, and honestly, it felt great. Then I met Michael at work. He was attending a class, and we got together with a few of my friends and a few of his and went to a club. It was an informal get-together, and it made me feel more comfortable not to be in the spotlight. He turned out to be fun to be with, and we were soon dating steadily.

After two years, we decided to get married. He was divorced, with two children of his own. Fortunately, Louis and Michael's two children got along well, and he was happy we would be a family. After we set the date, I bought a beautiful gown, chose six bridesmaids, and decided to have a big wedding, with the reception at a country club nearby.

To no one's surprise, my son, Louis, would be giving me away. Six-year-old Louis, in his gray tuxedo, walked down the aisle with me, and as I walked to the altar, he would not let go of my arm. He said, "I don't want to give you away. You're my mother!"

I looked at him calmly and said, "No one will ever take me away from you, because *you* are the love of my life and will be forever."

Happy with that argument, he finally removed his hand from my arm, but instead of sitting in his seat, he stood right there beside me during the entire ceremony, as proud as could be. I wouldn't have had it any other way.

9

A Second Chance

"I would like to learn, or remember how to live again…"

—*Annie Dillard*

After the wedding, Michael and I settled down and began living the life of a happily married couple. Immediately, the family grew by three: we would have Michael's two children every other weekend, and on alternating weeks during the summer. We were officially a "blended family," with new traditions, new personalities, new habits, and new schedules. Fortunately, Louis loved the fact that he had a new sister and brother to play with.

Michael also worked for the telephone company, so we had a lot in common when it came to discussing work during dinner or attending the various telephone-company functions that occurred throughout the year. It was a good fit for both of us, and I was determined to make it work, not just for myself and Michael, but especially for Louis.

By this time, Louis was in second grade. Although he was still acting up in school, he was doing well with his grades. As for myself, I was still working in Marlboro and doing well at my job. On weekends we would take the kids swimming at the local pool, or take day trips that left us sunburned and happy. Professionally and personally, I'd never been more content.

What continued to amaze me was the way my relationship with Louis remained as strong as ever, or maybe even stronger, with all the changes we'd been through with the new family dynamic. Though our life was busier now and fuller and new characters had been added to complement our world of two, Louis never missed an opportunity to express his love for me.

One day Louis came home with a bunch of beautiful flowers in his hand. He said, "These are for you, Mom. I picked them myself."

I bent down, picked him up, and said, "These are the most beautiful flowers I've ever seen, Louis. Where did you find them?"

Louis just smiled and said, "In the woods." I gave him a hug and a kiss and told him that I would keep them forever. I knew they would die eventually, but I hoped that with a child's short attention span, Louis wouldn't notice. For a while I kept them on the table, or sometimes I would bring them to work and put them beside the little drawings and things Louis would make me at school.

The flowers eventually died, and Louis would come home again from playing with other children in the complex, ring the doorbell, and as I opened the door I saw his hand behind his back. Out came…more flowers! I couldn't figure out what I admired more: his sensitivity or his ingenuity in always finding me fresh flowers just as his last batch was about to die out. He was always so proud of bringing me such beautiful flowers. He knew that flowers were one key to my heart.

As the middle of the summer approached and I was headed for work one morning, I stopped at the entrance to the condominium and glanced over at the flowers. They were all so pretty and colorful, but suddenly I noticed that something was missing. Bunches of flowers had been pulled up so that there were more spaces between each group. One thought came to mind: Louis! Apparently, he had been picking the flowers for me from the flower beds at the entrance to our complex. Now I had two options: I could tell him not to pick those particular flowers anymore and hurt his feelings, or I could just say nothing and enjoy them.

I said nothing. Even though I knew deep down that I should say something, I just couldn't. I knew I couldn't. How could I have looked Louis in the eyes and told him that bringing me happiness was wrong? I knew that one morning, there would be an empty flower garden, but at least it would have brought me happiness.

As Louis went through the first, second, and third grades in Westboro, I signed him up for all the sports they offered. There were a lot to choose from: soccer, basketball, baseball and hockey, and even snow-skiing. Sports in that town started as early as first grade. I thought, "Let's just get him involved in everything, and then he can decide which ones he enjoys the most."

It turned out that Louis excelled in basketball and hockey. In the second grade, he started playing baseball too. Once baseball season was in full swing, Michael and I went to every game, often taking Louis and his friends to

Friendly's restaurant for ice cream afterward. It became a weekly tradition, and it was one that I missed when the season finally ended that year.

My fears about becoming part of a blended family, playing favorites and choosing sides, turned out to be in vain. Michael was the perfect stepfather to Louis. He always supported him, making sure he was available for all of his games and especially school meetings, of which there were plenty. He was also involved in most of the decisions we made in raising Louis, and always supported me at every turn. It seemed I lived two lives now; even though I was married, I still felt it was just Lou and me. There just didn't seem to be that extra place in my heart for anyone else. I loved Michael and his children and treated them like family. They *were* family. But still, I just didn't feel the same about them as I did about Louis. Michael never challenged it. He had known from the beginning that if it came down to Louis or Michael, there would never be a choice.

Michael treated my boy like he was his own son, and Louis loved him in return. It was the best choice I could have made to ensure that Louis had a permanent male figure in his life. I knew time would bring us all together in a way that was equal, and that, until then, we would all just continue to work on it together.

The year was 1986 when we finally started looking for a piece of land. We were at my parents' house one night, talking about moving, and my father said, "Your mother and I have discussed this, and if you want to build behind us, we'll subdivide our lot and you can build a house there."

Their lot was an acre and a half in size. Michael and I jumped at the offer, and we started clearing the land and building a house right away. We moved into the house in the spring of 1987. We didn't have enough money to build both a garage and a pool; when it got down to selecting one or the other, there was no doubt in my mind: I chose the pool.

Lou was nine by now, and Michael's two children were nine and eleven. I knew that between work and paying the bills, our trips to the Cape would be limited, so the pool would be the next best thing.

Michael did a lot of the work himself, both inside and outside our new house. Lou was always there to help. Michael would give him small jobs to do while he concentrated on the woodwork, the wrap-around deck, another deck off my bedroom, a front walk, and all the other extras that don't come when the house is built. At long last, our new home was finished and we could begin to enjoy it as we settled into our new house.

Louis entered the fourth grade in Hopedale in the fall of 1987. After several years in which parent-teacher conferences and complaints about his behavior

were the norm, this was to be a banner year for Louis. He did well with his studies and found new friends. He formed a lasting friendship with his friend, Brett.
Brett would become his best friend for the next twelve years. They were in all the
same sports, and they formed a bond that was never broken. Lou would sleep
over at Brett's house and even go on trips with his family. I would have Brett over
for the weekend and take them shopping at the malls, swimming, or down to the
Cape for the day. Brett definitely became part of the family.

For me, living next to my parents was a big plus. They would watch Louis
when he came home from school, and I wouldn't have to worry about whether or
not the sitter showed or about dropping him off at day care or an after-school
program. Instead, he'd go over and watch TV some place safe and secure.

I had never been terribly close to my father, but over the next ten years, all
that changed. Because I lived behind them now, suddenly I was able to spend
more time renewing our relationship. I had always been closer to my mother, and
this gave me a chance to get closer to him for a change.

I found that because my mother had always been the stronger of the two, I
had always leaned more toward her whenever I'd had any problems while growing up. I saw a weakness in my father with which I guess I was just not comfortable. At that time in our lives, he would rather turn his head when there was a
problem than face it, so it was always my mother that shouldered all our problems. Mom was always listening and never judging, and giving us her strength.
But now I saw another side to my dad, and over the next decade, that bond
would grow stronger than ever.

He wasn't the only one. My sister, Gloria, was in high school now. She was a
straight-*A* student: another sister smarter than me. We were always close, and
became closer after I moved there.

She was popular and pretty, and everyone loved her. Since she was the youngest of all of us, my father had always called her "his baby." We, in turn, named
her "the princess." We had all spoiled her from the day she was born. She was
eleven years younger than Mike and me, and we doted on her and protected her
from anything that might put her in harm's way. She eventually became the
babysitter for Louis and Mike's two children, Jason and Jamie. The kids loved
her because she was young and they considered her one of them. In later years,
both Louis and Jamie would go to Gloria when they needed help with a problem,
or just to hang out with her. Gloria was not only an aunt to our kids, but also
their friend.

Michael and I were still getting along quite well. He was a good husband to
me. He treated me like I was a princess and was a great help with Louis. Once

again, I found peace in my life. I was especially glad that Louis loved Michael, and it gave me great comfort to know that the man I loved cared equally for the person I loved most: my son.

At around this time, a new flower store named Wildside Florist had opened around the corner from my house. I stopped in one day to introduce myself to the owner, a pleasant woman named Giselle. We had a nice talk about her new store, and we became fast friends.

The store's central location and its generous owner became a focal point of our family celebrations. On Mother's Day, my birthday, and other holidays, Louis would walk to the florist with all his change and ask Giselle what he could buy with the money he had. She would count the change and make up a beautiful arrangement that must have cost ten times what Lou had offered her. Lou would always ask for a pink or white rose, and she would put a piece of baby's breath in the arrangement, then off he would go to deliver my flowers and a card to me. I saved all of his cards over twenty years, and would one day be glad that I had.

One day, after doing errands Louis and I stopped at the florist to get some flowers. Giselle couldn't believe he was my son, and proceeded to tell me the story of the "holiday flowers." She said he was so cute coming up with all the change he had in his hands and that she always gave him a pink or white rose, knowing he didn't have enough money but it didn't matter to her; it was the thought that counted.

As the days and years went by, I was content. Work was going well, the marriage was fine, family life was improving, and we now had our dream house, but I always had a feeling that something was missing in my heart. I could never quite figure out what it was. It was almost a feeling that after all these years, something was still *missing*. I did love Michael, but I never felt I loved him enough or even the way a wife *should* love her husband. I always reflected on Charlie and our relationship, recalling that promise I had made to myself after he died that I would never love anyone as deeply as him. At the time, I had meant it. Maybe I still did. I thought time would change or heal that feeling, but it never did. A piece of my soul had been shattered, and I knew then I had lost a piece of myself.

I had locked the door to my heart, and, in doing so, I had lost that special love to give to another man. Yes, I would love again, but never the everlasting love I had for Charlie, the type that only comes once in a lifetime. I would accept that as the years passed. I would put aside my indifferent feelings for Michael and instead live my life not for myself, but for Louis, who was the only person who would ever have my heart. It was a decision I never regretted.

10

Crossroads

"There are years that ask questions and years that answer."

—*Zora Neale Hurston*

As the years went by, my only hope was that Louis would stay just like he was: handsome and polite, with tons of friends and even some girlfriends. In many ways, he seemed the one constant in my life as my sisters and my brother drifted apart, all of us attending to our own lives and children. We remained very close, and talked on the phone every week, sometimes even going out to eat or to the movies. But family and work took up most of our time. Mike went to school to become a respiratory therapist, Gloria was in college having a great time, and Joanie went to school and became a manicurist. And me? Well, I was still at the phone company, making so many lasting friendships along the way that I never regretted not going to college. I loved being back in Hopedale, where I'd grown up, and I still often saw old high-school friends.

Jack had moved to Phoenix by then, and I must admit we missed him terribly. He would come home at various times of the year, and we loved seeing him, but it just wasn't the same as it had been when we were growing up. Still, for those precious moments, it was once again Pat, Mike, and Jack—still as close as ever, with so many happy memories that even time could not take them away.

Jack wasn't the only one I was getting reacquainted with during this point of my life. I started getting closer to my father, and understanding him more over the years. He would often come over to the pool and was now the pool's official lifeguard. It was great to see him with the kids, and in many ways, I believe his grandchildren brought him even closer to his own children. It's funny how that works.

I also became more involved in working out and running in the morning, eventually going to school at night and getting certified with the Aerobics and Fitness Association of America, otherwise known as the AFAA, as an aerobics instructor. This was no fitness fad for me; years later I would go to school for personal training.

Even when it came to our health, mother and son were joined together, literally: Louis joined my health club, and after work, I would pick him up and we would go work out together. I would do aerobics while Louis would lift weights. It was just another great time for us, sharing more time together while having more adult conversations as our relationship evolved over time.

Of course, the protectiveness and jealousy Louis felt became stronger as he got older and learned what guys were *really* like. One night we were walking into the gym, and joking with him, I said, "Now remember, Louis, when we go into the gym, my name is 'Pat,' not 'Mom.'" True to form, he just laughed, but I would soon learn he was quite the selective listener.

Then again, I was always pretending to be younger than I was, to the point where it became a joke with the whole family and my work friends. One day, I said to him, "Louis, how old am I?"

Lou said, "Mom, I don't remember. I'll have to ask Auntie Mike."

As we worked out, he would be across the room doing his weights, watching all the time to see whom I talked to. If a guy came over to talk to me, Lou would be there in seconds, saying, "Mom, are you almost ready?" (So much for the calling me "Pat" part!)

We would get in the car afterward and laugh over our personal jokes. I soon realized that the fear he had of losing any part of me was intense. He wanted my undivided attention; he wanted my life to be devoted to him. Yes, it was my own fault for having put him first his entire life, but despite the inconvenience it meant to my dating life, that bond was something I never regretted. As long as he felt safe and secure, I was happy.

Through it all he had his friends—and a lot of girlfriends—and I had him. Once, down at the Cape, we were sitting on the beach, and it had been a long but beautiful summer day. As we watched the waves coming in, seagulls diving in the water for food, and looking at the shells we had collected, he said, "I love the ocean and the beach. One day I am going to buy you a house on the ocean and we'll live here: me, my wife, and you."

I said, "What about my boyfriend?"

He laughed and said, "You won't have any!"

I looked at him and said, "Promise?"

He hesitated and said, "Promise. I'm going to be very rich someday and that is the first thing I am going to buy for you." He was as serious as I had ever seen him. He would someday buy me that house, because he knew this was a dream I never thought would come true. And I knew it would be his way of giving back to me what I had given him all those years. I loved him so much at that moment, and if I never got my dream house, it would not be because he had forgotten that promise, it would be because he wasn't able to keep it.

Back at home, work was going well for me. I loved my job and the people who worked for me. Michael had been promoted to second level and was making good money. We were still getting along well, and the kids got along great together. Also, I was spending more quality time with my parents.

I was content, and hoping this period of peace, positively, and prosperity would last. As I became more involved with working out and health, I continued to go to my doctor once a year for my yearly check-up. In 1987, after my visit, my doctor called and asked me to come back in for another Pap smear. Naturally, I asked him why, and he said he wanted to recheck the results.

So the next week I went back, and two more times after that. Another call from him came a week later; he asked me to come to his office sometime that week along with Michael. I started getting nervous and asking all kinds of questions, but he wouldn't say anything until we got there. Once we were in his office, the doctor started to explain the readings of the four Pap smears he had taken over the past two weeks. Apparently every result had been different, but there was really only one reading that mattered: the last one revealed that I had cervical cancer, but if treated immediately, my chances of a full recovery were good.

He made me an appointment with an oncologist for the next week. The oncologist would go in and scrape the walls of my uterus to remove the cancerous cells, and then I would have surgery with my own doctor.

I was strong on the surface. I never told Louis about it, but I was very upset and nervous about the prospects of the procedure. Just the thought of dying at such a young age was unthinkable to me. It seemed like a pattern with me: just when things were finally going well, tragedy would strike. It wasn't even the fear of fighting cancer, or, for that matter, losing the fight. The fact was that I simply wasn't ready to die and leave Louis behind. I had too much to do for him. But using the strength my mother had taught me, I went to work and continued my everyday routine as normally as I possibly could. After surgery, my doctor told me it would take three months to see the results.

A very long and anxious ninety days went by. I went back to the doctors, had another test, and waited for the results. A week later, my doctor called and said the results were great, but that I would have to have a Pap smear four times a year for five years, just to ensure the cancer did not return. Thankfully, he had caught it in time, and after five years, I was finally given a clean bill of health. I still went twice a year for a check-up for my own peace of mind, but things were fine, so after ten years I went back to once a year. Amazingly, God had given me another chance. He knew my work was not done on this earth. After all, I still had Louis to raise.

In 1989, I was up for a promotion at work. There were no jobs available in Marlboro, so I had a choice: I could either go to Boston to work (which on a good day with no traffic would be an hour each way, with limited parking) or to Brockton, which was still an hour-long drive, but I wouldn't be in the infamous Boston traffic jams and accidents that continually occurred on the highway.

In the end I chose Brockton, but I was heartbroken to leave my job and all the friends I had made over those fourteen years. Still, the promotion seemed to me to be an omen of some kind. I knew it was time to move on. There is a time when you get too comfortable on a job, and life seems to pass you by, as you move inevitably through the rut in which you find yourself.

The promotion meant an increase in pay, and the new job would be totally different from what I was doing at the time. I would have "field people" working for me. Also, the new position was a job I had no experience in. It was definitely going to be a challenge for me. So, after the going-away parties, I started work in Brockton on July 7, 1989.

As with any time when a new supervisor comes in to replace the old one, I was tested by the people that worked for me. Unfortunately, they had already been told I had no field experience, and these folks were considered a tough group of union employees. As I started to learn my job, working with other supervisors and working with my reporting people, it was often an uncomfortable situation. I had left behind many close friends, to come to another job with no friends, to prove to myself—and my co-workers—that I would learn, and be as knowledge-able as they were. Unfortunately, that would have to wait.

What did happen on August 10, four weeks after I had started working there, the union contract expired. After long negotiations, the union members went out on strike. It was the longest one I had ever experienced, which lasted a total of three and a half months. As if that wasn't bad enough, I had to cross the picket line every morning, driving by the very people that, just a few weeks earlier, had worked for me! It was a feeling I never wanted to have again. Not only were these people not getting paid, but they would be back in and working for me again when it was all over.

To make matters worse, Louis was only twelve at the time. Michael was also in management, so he would be working in the Boston area. Suddenly both of us were working twelve-hour days, seven days a week, with one day off after the third week. My hours were six to six, with an hour-long drive each way. As a result, Louis spent a lot of time with my parents, and I spent a lot of time missing him. That was the rest of our summer and fall, until early in November, when the union accepted a new contract. The following day, everyone was back at work, and I started getting to know my reporting people all over again.

As the days and months went by, we became co-workers, but also became friends. They helped me learn about their jobs, and I, in return, worked hard to gain their trust. For the next two years, the job got better every day. But at the same time as my relationships at work began to flourish, my relationship with Michael started to deteriorate.

My answer was to seek comfort in the best relationship I had at the time. As a result, I spent more time with Louis, going shopping, watching movies, and attending school events, all the while pretending my marriage was going to get better. As much as we both tried, though, Michael and I knew it was finally over.

I felt extremely sad about the deterioration of this marriage because I had loved Michael dearly during our ten years together. He had become Louis's second father, had been a wonderful, caring husband to me, and had made such a positive effect on my son while he was growing up. Michael had loved Lou as though he were his own son, and my son had loved him in return, even taking his name as his confirmation name, after which I bought him a chain with a cross on it as a gift. He never took it off.

It was one of the most difficult decisions I had to make, and worse yet was explaining to Lou why another marriage wasn't going to work. Louis took it fairly well, and Michael assured him he would always remain a part of his life.

Our divorce, unlike my last one, was friendly, as we discussed privately what we both thought was fair. We brought an agreement to my lawyer, and the divorce was granted six months later. Another chapter in my life closed, but this one was harder to accept. I made a decision at that point never to get married again. Now fourteen, Louis had been given a lot of love and support and had learned the important steps in becoming his own person. He would survive, and once more it was Louis and me against the world, only this time it really *would* be just the two of us—forever.

After the divorce, we remained in the house and continued with our lives. The saddest and most difficult part to handle was that after a few months of Louis calling Michael just to talk, we never heard or saw Michael again. We both learned another lesson: people change, and with change comes loss. We had officially lost Michael. We had each other, and that was it. I would be there for Louis whenever he needed me, and no one else would get close to us again. I thanked God that we had remained so close, even though other people had entered—and exited—our lives.

If I was the only one Louis could totally depend on, if he knew I would love him unconditionally, without any hesitation, and that he would still be my life, no matter what, I was content with that. Unfortunately, kids change too.

One day, Louis went to the mall with his cousin Shawn. Shawn had his driver's license, so off they went for the day. Louis came home with a present for me. It was a gold rope bracelet. It was the kind they pull off a cart, measure, cut, then attach the clasp. He was so proud of it, and as for me, I loved it. I put it on and told him I would never take it off. The bracelet stayed on my wrist for the next thirteen years.

Louis entered high school. Although Brett was still his best friend, he had also started hanging around with a different group of guys. His grades started dropping; he went from being a *B* student to being a *C* student. He had been diagnosed with attention deficit disorder when he had been in grammar school, so every night after I got home from work, I would sit at the table and help him do his homework. This went on for years, until he got older and decided that he was old enough to work on his homework alone. Unfortunately, his grades did not reflect this. Although he had never been disrespectful to me, suddenly Louis started to think he was old enough to hang out with his friends every night. I told him he could only go out on weekends until he was a little older. He didn't like that decree one bit, but accepted it nonetheless—for a few years, anyway.

Louis was extremely popular with the girls, but he really wasn't interested in any long relationships, about which I was secretly glad. I told him to enjoy his freedom, and that there would be plenty of time to settle down with one girl when he got older. One night, he came home and said he had met a girl from Milford named Nicole. I said, "That's nice," and promptly forgot all about it. Louis obviously didn't. On weekends he would go over to her house, or he would have her over. They would talk for hours on the phone, until I insisted he be off the phone by nine o'clock. Thank God for two phone lines!

We continued working out together, and he continued his relationship with Nicole. I loved her from the first time I met her. She was taller than Louis, and thin, with brown hair. As much as I loved her, he was still young and spending way too much time with her, so we finally discussed it one night. I suggested that he spend more time with other girls and his friends, especially Brett, who I considered a positive influence. But Louis was stubborn; he cared for Nicole more than any other girl he had been with, and he let me know it in no uncertain terms, so I just let it go.

After two productive years in Brockton, I accepted a job in Framingham as a field supervisor. I hated leaving my friends once again, but the commute back and forth from the new job would only be a half-hour and would give me more time to spend at home. So once again, after a great farewell party, I had to say goodbye to not only my co-workers, but friends I had made along the way. One woman in particular, Barbara, would remain my friend throughout the years.

In February 1992, I started my new job. The job was similar to the one I'd had in Brockton, but it was also an engineering office. I started to learn about the people who would be working for me. I sat with them and discussed their job descriptions, while also learning the jobs for which they were responsible. I was able to spend more time at home; I worked out as much as ever and was still able to be home by around five for supper. It was a welcome relief to have more free time, and a great change from the longer hours and the long commute to Brockton.

I met the same people every morning for coffee at eight am, wonderful people who became my best and closest friends: Scott, Bobby, Ciampi, Ronnie, Paul, and Lenny. (It didn't matter that I was the only girl!) We called it "The Breakfast Club," and it was the best part of my day. As the years went by, we became extremely close and very protective of each other, often socializing together on weekends along with our significant others. Years later, when tragedy struck, I leaned on them for support, and they had a big part in my recovery. Their loyalty, strength, and friendship are traits I will always cherish.

My parents still helped with Louis after he got out of school, but as he got older, he would come home, do his homework, and then go over to Brett's for a while. The next two years went along well, even though I had started spending more time at school meetings because of Lou's behavior or missing homework. I felt I was keeping on top of everything. 1994 proved me wrong.

Louis started getting in trouble at night. At first it was the normal things kids do when they are starting to feel independent, but as time went on, the normal things turned into more serious things like drinking and driving. Lou had gotten his license by now and was able to use my car on some important occasions. I didn't have the money to buy him a car, and when I realized he was drinking, I was glad I hadn't.

He had several jobs during high school, working at a grocery store, mowing lawns, doing construction work, and that sort of thing, but he was never able to keep a job long enough to save much money and buy his own car. He would call me every day when he got out of school just to check in and promise me that his homework was done, and then he would promptly go out.

One spring night, I got a call from the local police; Louis had been stopped for drinking while driving and had been arrested. The following day, we went to court, and Lou was put on six months' probation. His license was taken away for thirty days. In September 1994 he was arrested again, this time for driving under the influence and driving without a license. He had borrowed a friend's car. Once again, we went to court. Because this was his second offense, and he had violated probation and resisted arrest, he was sent to Springfield, a youth correctional facility, for three months.

As I sat in the courtroom and listened to his sentence, we looked at each other; Louis had a look of disbelief in his eyes, and I had tears in mine. The court officer brought him down to the holding cell to wait for the van that would take him to Springfield. A feeling of complete emptiness went through me. We had never been apart for any length of time, and now it would be three months!

I had to see him before I left. I just couldn't let them take my son without saying good-bye, not for so long, so I asked the court officer if I could just see him for a minute. Normally, no one other than court officials is allowed in the holding cell, but because I knew the officer, he allowed me to go down to say good-bye.

As I walked down the hall to the cell, I looked at my son and fought to keep back the tears, knowing there would be plenty of time for that later. As I approached, he stood up and put his hands through the bars. I could see that he was scared, and it was the first time I had ever seen him like that. So tough was this kid, nothing was ever going to happen to him, but when it did, his immaturity showed right through.

I tried to control my own feelings while holding his hands. I told him how much I loved him and asked him to call me as soon as he could. I promised I would come and see him every week, no matter what, and then I had to leave. I turned my head back once before I rounded the corner, but he had already sat down, totally defeated and unable to believe he was going to a correctional facility for minors. As I left the courthouse and walked toward my car, I let the tears flow, wishing this was just a dream and that it would all end, but I knew that sometimes the end is only the beginning of things to come.

My family was a constant support system for me during this turbulent time. By visiting often and calling constantly to see if I was doing all right, they were my life support and connection to the real world. There was nothing anyone could say to make it easier or less embarrassing to deal with, but they were always there to lend an ear or offer whatever help I needed.

My friends at work and my reporting people were thoughtful and understanding enough not to say the wrong words or mention what had happened. I thanked God every day for the constant support and friendship that was given to me at work, making it less difficult to get up every morning to take on another day. My strategy became to walk with my head held high and a smile on my face, regardless of the situation. It was something that would eventually become a part of my everyday life and personality as a result of what happened one fateful spring night.

As the days went by, I buried myself in my work, spent more time at the gym, visited with my family, and waited for Lou's calls at home. He was always anxious to talk. There was a TV in the game room he called from. I would usually be watching Wheel of Fortune, so he would turn on the same channel and we would play the game together. We would talk about our days, and then it would be time to hang up. I was able to visit him twice a week. I would leave right from work, driving an hour and a half each way, just to see him for an hour. Regardless of the hassle, we both looked forward to those two days.

Usually one of my sisters, my mother, or my sister-in-law would come with me on Saturdays, which gave me company and gave Louis another visitor. He really wanted to see some of his friends, and couldn't understand why they never showed up. I would come up with excuses—it was too long a drive, they had homework, whatever popped into my mind at the moment—anything but the truth. Life hadn't stopped when Louis had gone to Springfield. People went on with their lives, and Louis would just have to catch up when he got out. Every few weeks, I would meet with his counselor to discuss his progress. His teachers were kind enough to send his books and homework up to Springfield, so he would be able to keep up with his studies.

Finally, just before Christmas, Louis was released. As we drove home that chilly December morning, he was surprised to see snow on the trees. He had gone away in early fall, and now it was winter. The first thing he wanted to do was to go to breakfast, and then to the mall. Christmas was Lou's favorite holiday, with all the lights and festivities and being surrounded by people shopping in the stores. I was happy to make him feel a part of that once more, to give him the feeling that he had never been away. So we ate breakfast, and went shopping, and once we got back home, he went over to see my mother and father then went off to Brett's house, where he stayed for a few hours to catch up on all the news around town. I would save the long discussion we needed to have about his future for after Christmas and my birthday. For now, I was just glad he was home. I didn't want to ruin the feeling for either of us. 1995 would be a better year for both of us; I just knew it.

After the holidays, Louis had a week off for school vacation, and I had taken a vacation week so I could spend time with him. Lou slept late, I cooked breakfast or lunch (depending on the time he woke up), and then he went off with his friends. One afternoon, I caught him between visits, and we sat down and discussed his stay in Springfield, the mistakes he had made, and, most importantly, whether he had learned from them. He assured me that he had, so the discussion ended. Lou always had the best intentions; he was sensitive, caring, always concerned for my feelings, and never wanted to hurt me. But I was always waiting for the other shoe to drop. The rest of the school year went well for him, and it appeared as though he had learned from his mistakes, because he managed to stay out of trouble.

I had started seeing Tony, a man with whom I worked. We had gone out to dinner once in a while when Lou had been in Springfield, but at the time, it was just as friends. I had been dating another guy at the time, while Tony had also been in another relationship. But it was nice to talk to someone with whom I wasn't involved. Tony was another shoulder to lean on while Louis was at Springfield.

At the time, I wasn't interested in getting serious with anyone. I was quite independent at this time in my life. I had adjusted to having my own life and my own space, and a commitment to anyone was the farthest thing from my mind. I enjoyed doing what I wanted without answering to anyone, except perhaps to Louis. Lou didn't care about any of my boyfriends; he knew they wouldn't last very long and were never involved with us or took any time away from him, so as far as he was concerned, everything was fine.

Nicole was still dating Lou. Lou was spending more time with his friends, and working during the summer. He enjoyed the pool, and what would end up being his last "free summer." He would call to see if I was in the pool on weekends, and if I was, he'd want to know what time I would be out. He wanted to bring his friends over, but didn't want them seeing me in my bathing suit. The older he got, it seemed, the more jealous he was. One of his friends had told him once how cool and pretty I was and how lucky he was to have me as a mother. That was all Louis needed to hear. From then on, none of his friends ever made a comment like that again. I remember Brett saying to me once, "It doesn't matter who it is; they know better than pay you any kind of a compliment in front of Louis."

Around this time I started to notice a difference in Lou's attitude and personality. I couldn't quite figure out what it was, but something was different, and it wasn't anything positive. He'd come home from school, sleep, and then go out with friends or Nicole. I soon learned what the change was: he had started drinking again. I could smell it on him when he came home. When confronted with this, of course, Lou would just say, "I only had one beer."

Then the day came when I found pot under the couch, concealed in a paper bag, along with papers to roll it with. I sat down to think about what I was going to do and how I would approach him about this recent discovery. When he walked in the door later that day, I simply held up the bag and watched the reaction on his face. The smile was immediately replaced with a somber look. I didn't even have to ask; immediately, I knew all I needed to know. I flushed it down the toilet, and once again I had a long talk with Lou about how dangerous drugs were and how they led to other, worse things. He had just gotten his license back, but as a result of everything he'd gotten into recently I still would not let him drive my car. I even brought him to counseling, where he answered all the questions the doctor asked him. Typical Louis—he agreed with everything and said all the right things, which eventually got him out of a situation he didn't want to be in.

I was now dating Tony. We had both ended our previous relationships and slipped right into dating. Unfortunately, the timing was not conducive to romance, and our new, official relationship was a constant roller-coaster ride, with Lou as the focus of my problems. Tony did his best to understand, knowing Louis was definitely in a place in his life that he shouldn't have been at such a young age. All the while, I felt I was totally alone with my problems, and I was too embarrassed, most of the time, to tell anyone how much trouble Louis was really getting into.

Now the principal called on a monthly basis about Lou's behavior, or, if not that, it was his lack of interest in his schoolwork and his grades going down. Finally, the principal called to inform me that my son was at risk of repeating his junior year! That summer, he ended up going to summer school and taking two classes, just to get into his senior year.

As he started his senior year in 1995, it was all I could do to make sure his homework was done and his behavior improved; all the while I was watching for drugs and alcohol to pop up in one of Lou's mysterious hiding places.

On New Year's Eve, he asked to borrow my car. I had just bought a new Toyota in October. We had planned to spend New Year's Eve at home, with Brett coming over later that night. He begged me to take the car just downtown and then to pick up Brett, and I finally agreed, but told him to be back in an hour.

The hour turned into three. All of a sudden, the door opened, and in came Louis. I knew my car was not in the driveway. As Louis walked up the stairs, I asked him what had happened, and he said, "I slid on black ice, but the car is all right; it just had to be towed to fix the tire." I made sure both Lou and Brett were all right, and I realized that I would be in for a long wait to hear about the damage to my car. The holiday fell on a Monday, and I wouldn't be able to get any information until Tuesday.

On Tuesday, I borrowed my mother's car to go to work, and called the garage. Fix a tire? Yeah, *right* My new car had been totaled. Not only had Lou slid on black ice, he had plowed into an embankment, demolishing everything underneath the car. As I hung up the telephone, all I could do was cry. I was at a point with Lou where I couldn't quite comprehend what my son had put us through over the past few years, and this, it seemed, was my breaking point. When I told Louis about the car, his reaction was at first disbelief. Then he apologized, telling me how truly sorry he was. Finally, he made a toss-off remark that at least the car was insured.

In March of Lou's senior year, he decided to quit school, and simply walked home.

When the principal called me, I immediately hung up the phone and left work. I went home and saw Louis sitting on the couch, watching television. I asked him what was going on. He said that he wasn't going back and he didn't care about graduating. He was going to be eighteen in May, and he just didn't care. In fact, Lou didn't care about much of anything by that point in his life.

All the nights and years of making sure his homework was done, all those school meetings and progress reports had been useless. He had instead focused on drinking, drugs, and partying with his friends. There was nothing I could do at that point. I couldn't reason with him, much less have any kind of adult conversation. Louis continued on his road of self-destruction while I sat in the background, helpless, because there was nothing I could do for him. In August 1995, he was arrested again for breaking and entering, possession of illegal drugs, and drinking.

Once again I found myself sitting in court, waiting to hear his sentence. The setting might have been the same, but the circumstances were now quite different. He had violated his probation again, and this sentence would be much more serious than the last one. He would be sent to the Worcester House of Correction until his sentencing date. Once again, I saw on Lou's face the same look of disbelief, only this time, I almost thought he looked a little relieved. I knew he couldn't get control of his life, so maybe this was what it would take. I also knew that, at this point, I couldn't help him do it either. My feelings were a mix of emotions that day. Maybe going away would straighten him out, would let him think about his life and which direction he wanted to go. I also knew that this was not the life he wanted to lead. He desperately wanted to succeed and make something of himself, yet every time he had the opportunity to do this, it just never happened. It was almost as though if anything good happened in his life, he made sure to destroy it.

What hurt most of all was that this was not the son I had raised, and I really did not understand why he did the things he did. With only the clothes he was wearing, and a backward glance to me, he was led by the court officer back to the holding cell. Only this time, I didn't beg, barter, or cash in my chips to get a secret trip back there. Instead, I left the courthouse, got into my car, and went straight home. I sat in my living room for what seemed like hours and thought about nothing at all. I just sat and stared at the television, not really watching, not really listening, just eager for some kind of distraction.

Tomorrow was no longer an opportunity; tomorrow was just another day.

Louis called me a few days later. He had discovered that his new home away from home certainly wasn't like Springfield. He was now in with drug dealers and real criminals. His voice cracked a little while we talked. I had called up to Worcester to see when visiting hours were, and had again learned the routine: twice a week, no shorts, no halter tops, no dresses, no jewelry, no pocketbook, and so on.

As I sat in the parking lot, waiting to go in to visit with Louis for the first time and dreading it inside, I thought, *I can do this. I have to; he's my son.* In I walked, up to the desk, where I gave my name and told whom I was visiting. Then I heard the familiar refrain: "Have a seat. You'll be called when he is down in the recreation room."

As I looked around the waiting room, I saw so many different types of people—mothers, fathers, sisters, brothers—all with the same look that I felt rested on my own face. It was a look of defeat, betrayal, and bewilderment. At that moment, I knew I looked just like them, waiting to be called to visit my son, anxious for him to hurry down, so I could get in and give him a hug.

When the security guard finally called my name, I stood up, went through security, and was led to another waiting room, where I would stay until Louis was seated at the table. I finally got in and hugged my son, just as the guard told me, "No touching." We sat down and Louis started to talk. I looked around the room at the other inmates and their families; there was laughter from some tables, concern at others, and just plain "Do I have to be here?" looks at other tables.

Louis looked like such a young boy compared to the men I was seeing. He was eighteen, but still had that boyish look to him. I was afraid that the unthinkable would happen. I couldn't concentrate on any kind of conversation. I tried to act as if nothing was wrong and that I didn't have a clue about what went on in jail, and Louis never confirmed that from the first day he got there, he had found out the rules very quickly.

Instead we played some cards and talked about fun things, and I told him that I would bring Nicole up the next time I visited. When it was time to leave, he asked me to put some money "on the books" for him. This jail slang meant leaving money at the desk with the guard so he could get soap, a toothbrush, some food, and cigarettes. They weren't allowed to have any money. I told him that I would, and gave him one more hug and a kiss, and then, just like that, he left. I watched him walk through the door, and saw him standing there with two guards. The reason was chilling: He would be strip-searched every time he had a visit.

Louis was eventually sentenced to eight months to a year in prison. I couldn't decide whether it was more or less than what I'd expected. As he served his sentence, life simply went on. I would visit twice a week, with my family, Nicole, or some of his friends. Another six months of his life was wasted in jail. Every time he got out, Lou would go back to being the child I had raised: so sensitive, so caring, and always promising it would be the last time. But it wasn't.

He had grown up this time, and came out with a tattoo around his ankle that some guy had done for him in jail. Another night, he came home with one on his arm. I told him that was enough—he was starting to look like he *belonged* in jail. He went to night school and received his GED. Once more, things started going well for him.

He started doing construction work, and I continued dating Tony. Gloria had gotten married and was living in Uxbridge. She was working for a cable company, and Jamey, her husband, was also doing construction work. My parents were doing well. My job was great; I worked with close friends who were also my support system. I had met Tony's family, which consisted of three sons, their wives, his sisters, and his father. We started spending more time together, attending joint family functions and holidays, and going on trips to the beach.

Tony was also a diver, so we would meet his son in Lowell and drive to Gloucester. While Tony, his son, and his nephews dove for lobsters, Michele (Tony's daughter-in-law) and I would read, get some sun, and catch up. We always joked with the guys that if they didn't come back with plenty of lobsters, they weren't getting back in the boat. So along with the bad, there were also good times. Louis and I would still go shopping once a week, then out to the movies or dinner. He spent more time with Nicole and his friends, and stayed out of trouble for a while.

In October 1996 Louis was arrested once again for resisting arrest, possession of an illegal substance (cocaine), disorderly conduct, and driving under the influence of liquor. This time he was sentenced to eighteen months in Worcester, of which he would serve at least a year. The first time I went back up to visit, I told Louis exactly how I felt: he was ruining his life, had broken my heart, and even though I loved him, I just didn't *like* him.

He simply couldn't understand what that meant, so I explained to him that sometimes you can love someone very much, but dislike their actions at the same time. It was embarrassing for both of us. I told him I didn't know when I would be back up again. I knew no one else would be visiting him or leaving money for cigarettes, soap, or food, but I didn't care at that point. I needed some time to sort things out and figure out what it was that made him try to destroy and hurt everything good in his life over and over again.

Years later, my sister Gloria would tell me a story about something that happened during this time, a story that touched my heart and broke it, all at the same time. She spoke about a time when she had pulled into a local convenience store and noticed that Louis was sitting in the passenger's seat in the car right next to her. Although they had been close, she hadn't seen or heard from him in a while, and she had been concerned about how he was, and what was going on with him. Unfortunately, the answers to those questions were not ones she wanted to hear.

She had first tried to get his attention by playing a little joke with him and throwing little pebbles from her car floor into the window of the car in which he was sitting. She had soon realized, however, that he was oblivious to what she was doing. She had called his name once, but had gotten no response. She had called it louder, and finally he had looked up with a blank stare.

When she had seen how he looked, so empty and unresponsive, she had realized that things weren't going well for him. After a few minutes, it had finally dawned on him who he was looking at, and he had smiled and said hi, with an almost desperate tone in his voice. Then Lou had gotten out of the car and gone over and kissed her.

She had asked how things were going, and he had actually told her "Not well." She had been able to tell by his messy hair, his dirty clothes, his scruffy face, and his pale color that this was quite the understatement. He had always been a very neat and clean boy, and it had broken her heart to see him this way. He had been almost rambling, as if he couldn't get his words out fast enough, and all the while he'd kept looking for the driver of the car to come out of the store.

She said he had been playing with the cross around his neck, the one that I had given him, throughout the whole conversation. She had asked what was going on with him and why he looked so bad. He had said he knew he was not taking care of himself, and partying too much, and had seemed almost desperate for it to stop. He had said his life was out of control and that he had sold everything he owned to buy drugs. He had also said that he felt he had no power to change things, but that he'd had a conversation with me the day before, and had promised to get back on track. He'd said he had only one thing left that was worth anything, and although he didn't want to, he felt compelled to sell it, have one last good time, and then do whatever he had to do to get his life back on track.

The one thing he'd had left, of course, was the cross I had bought him for confirmation. He'd told Gloria he had held onto it and refused to sell it because his mother had given it to him and it was the only thing he had that really meant anything to him. He'd said it was going to kill him, but that he was on his way to a friend's house to see someone that was going to give him a hundred dollars for the cross and chain, and that he would use this for his "last good time."

The monetary value of the chain and cross was probably four times that amount, and its sentimental value was simply priceless. Gloria had asked him several times not to do it, but she'd realized that something else was controlling his actions, and that no matter what she said, he was determined to do this desperate, final act. She'd known he would regret it the second he did it; he'd seemed to know this, too, and that there would be no undoing the deed.

What she had done next was against everything she felt was right inside, except the hope that one day, hopefully soon, Lou would gain control of his life and he would still have that one thing that actually did mean something to him. She'd told him that she would give him the hundred dollars for the chain and the cross, and that someday, when he did straighten his life out, she would give it back to him as a reminder of where he had been and what he had accomplished to earn back the chain.

He had seemed relieved, in more ways than one. She reluctantly gave him the hundred dollars, kissed him goodbye, and told him that no matter what time he needed to call her, she would help him in any way she could. As he had driven off, she had hoped she had done the right thing and that she would never have to tell me that she had contributed to something potentially bad. She had known she could never live with that.

Lou would call, and I continued to be distant with him. Finally, after two weeks of self-imposed exile, I went back up to visit him. He was definitely happy to see me, and said all the right things. He said he was so sorry he had hurt me, which he hadn't meant to, but it had just happened. It was hard to believe anything he said, but in my mind, I at least gave him an *A* for effort.

The holidays were coming up, and it would be the first Christmas he would not be home. I didn't put up a tree or decorate, like I had for the last nineteen years of his life. It was just too much for me, and I wasn't in a mood to celebrate. On Christmas Day, Tony, my mother, and I went up in the afternoon to visit him.

He seemed to be in good spirits, and I tried not to cry or say anything that would make him sad. As we were leaving, he told me to wait in the car for five minutes. His room faced the parking lot, so he would be able to wave good-bye. We waited in the car, and then I saw his face in the window—a window with bars on it. He looked like such a little boy, waving to us from his room. I cried all the way home. *What has happened to him?* I wondered. *Why is God doing this to us?* It was one of the saddest moments of my life. I saw his face in that window for a long time.

One day, I went up to visit. I had become friendly with the security guard at the desk; it was like we were old friends. But there was someone new working the security box that day. As I walked through, the buzzer went off. I went back through twice before the guard said, "Go sit down. You will have to be searched."

Dave, my friend, said, "She's fine; let her go through," but the guard insisted on me being searched. Dave called a female guard, and I was brought into a room and searched. She found nothing, and apologized for the inconvenience.

Meanwhile, Louis had been waiting for me in the recreation room. When he finally saw me, I told him what had happened. He went out of his mind. Louis told me not to come up again—he didn't want me to go through what he had to endure every time he got a visitor. I continued to go and see him, but never got searched again.

One night, he said, "I have to tell you something." The look on his face told me that I wasn't going to like it. He said, "I got another tattoo, but you're going to like this one." He pulled his pant leg up. On his thigh, just above his knee, I saw the word *MOM* with two pink roses underneath. Now, I knew I should have been mad, but how could I be? He was grinning, and I looked at him and said, "That's nice."

Lou said, "I knew you'd like it."

He was released after a year. As I picked him up, I knew he would not be back. I would make sure this time. The telephone company was hiring technicians, and he was due to get his license back again. I told him about it on the way home and asked if he was interested in taking the test. He said yes right away, so I made an appointment for him to take the test in Boston. We both went in, and I prayed he would pass. After forty-five minutes, he came out. I asked how he had done, and he said that it hadn't been difficult at all. I knew for certain that he had failed. Usually, only two out of thirty would pass.

We waited for the testers to come out. One by one, they called in the candidates, gave them their results, and then watched them walk out. Louis was called last. He had passed! I stood up, gave him a kiss and a hug, and told him how proud I was. He was beaming from ear to ear. He was so proud of himself. He had finally kept his promise. He had done it more for himself than for me.

On the way in, I had made the mistake of telling him that I would buy a chain for him if he passed. Once again, I had to keep my promise. Louis looked at me and said, "Okay, where's the closest jewelry store?" Even though I didn't have the money, I bought Louis another gold chain. He would start eight weeks of school in July 1997, and then he would work in the Framingham garage as a technician. It was the same office where I worked.

I threw a party for Louis, his friends, and family to celebrate his accomplishment, complete with a cake decorated with a telephone man on a telephone pole. It was a great party, but the best gift he received was from Gloria. She gave him back his chain with the cross, knowing full well that he now deserved it back. As he put it around his neck, his eyes filled with tears, remembering how desperate he had been—and realizing how far he had come.

That summer proved to be the best time of his life. He was the happiest I'd ever seen him. He was proud of himself, and had a great job with benefits to look forward to, as well as making excellent money. Every day, he'd come home from school and we'd sit and talk about his day. Now we had a lot more in common. I understood the kind of training he was getting, and he finally understood what kind of work I did.

He would go out with his friends or Nicole at night and have a great time. One night I got a call at eleven-thirty, and of course Tony and I had been sleeping. It was Louis asking me to come to a club he was at so he could buy me a drink. I told him it was too late, and I heard the disappointment in his voice, but I hung up anyway.

About five minutes later, Tony said, "Okay, get dressed and we'll meet up with him." When I walked into the club, Lou ran over to me, so happy that I had come, and gave me a hug and a kiss. His friends were there, so Tony and I sat with them and stayed until closing. Louis was so different: so happy, so proud. He was the son I knew and loved, so handsome with his blue eyes and beautiful smile. It was so great to see him like that, and I wished the night would never end. If there was a moment in time I wanted to stop, it was right there and then.

My wish for my son had finally come true. He was in a wonderful place in his life and in his heart; it seemed that all the tough times were behind him now. Lou continued to call different times at night, and Tony and I would go out and meet him. I figured that if he wanted his mother to hang out with him and his friends, I was going to be there.

When his training ended in August, he started his first day as a technician. I brought him to work, introduced him to his new supervisor, and left to go to my office. He blended right in with the other guys he worked with. He learned quickly, and everyone loved him. I co-signed for a Jeep for him to drive, knowing he would now be able to make the payments. Suddenly, all was good.

Summer turned into fall and fall into winter. One night just before Christmas, Louis was arrested for drinking and driving, possession of drugs, and threatening a police officer. I bailed him out once again, not believing this was happening. Since it was in the paper the next night, when Lou got to work, he was fired.

His union steward came up to see me, and told me he had done everything he could to save his job, but driving a company truck after being arrested was grounds enough to be fired. He asked me to come downstairs, which I did, and the steward took Lou's tools, keys, and company ID and was told to leave the building. As we walked out to the car, I didn't say a word. I had looked at him in the office and seen tears in his eyes. When he got into the car, he was crying. I think that, even with all he'd been through in the past, it was one of the worst times in his life. He knew he had just destroyed his career, and the look I had seen on his face a few months before was suddenly gone.

How right I was. I would never see it again, and Lou would never have that feeling again. He had destroyed what had made him the happiest he'd ever been, and he had no one to blame but himself. He had chosen the road of self-destruction, and that would be his life from that day on.

He went to court in January, where his charges were continued without a finding. He was put back on probation for another year, and he lost his license for ten years. I went back to work a few days later with my head held amazingly high, considering the embarrassment I felt, which was almost beyond belief. Again, everyone at work was great. My friends supported me with their undying understanding and concern. My family stuck by me, but most of them were so disappointed in Louis that it was hard for them to talk to him.

Instead, he went to Gloria with his problems. At least he had someone to talk with. His friends didn't care; they would always be his friends, no matter what happened. This time, Louis knew there was no way out, no way to go back and change things, and especially no way to repair the hurt he had caused me.

As the days passed, we talked about his future, and he decided to look for a job where he wouldn't have to drive. I tried to regain some kind of understanding and compassion for my son. It was a constant battle. He started working for another construction company that tore down buildings and then remodeled them. His boss knew he didn't have a license, but hired him anyway. Louis was a hard worker; in the end, I suppose, that's what mattered the most.

He'd call me at work when he was in Framingham to see if we could have lunch. He started coming home drunk, having stopped after work with the guys. I knew he was back on drugs again, although I never had any idea how bad it had become. Some nights he would come home so drunk and stoned that I'd lock my door when I went to sleep because I just didn't know what might happen. He was beyond being in control of himself, and I worried what he might do. Never in a million years could I ever have imagined locking my own son out of my room at night, but in the end, that's exactly what happened. I just didn't know what else to do when he was like that.

I was just thankful that he wasn't able to drive. This went on for months, until one night he called me to pick him up at his boss's house. It was November 23, 1998. He crossed the street, and running around the back of my car, he was hit by a car, thrown onto the hood of my car, and landed on the road face down. I jumped out of my car, feeling time had stopped, and ran over to Louis.

I didn't dare move him, but I held on to him instead, trying to see if he could talk, and assuring him I was there, which I felt was the most important thing he needed to hear at the moment. I tried to comfort him but also myself as I held his hand, hoping I would feel some type of movement, but I never did.

Somewhere in the distance I heard the sound of an ambulance, followed shortly thereafter by police cruisers and fire trucks. My thoughts went back to a time twenty-five years ago, not quite two miles up the same road. Here I was again, only this time, I was looking down at my son.

He was lying face down with his right arm across his face. His arms and legs appeared to be broken and were in an unnatural position, like that of a marionette whose strings had been cut and who had just fallen. His shirt was over his head, and his sneakers were off to the side of the road.

As the tears poured out of me, soaking the pavement with my pain, I looked at Lou's face. It was so peaceful, so beautiful and serene, but as I put my hand on his cheek, I saw blood surrounding his head. At that very moment, I begged God to take my life instead of my son's. I had lived my life, but Louis hadn't accomplished what he needed to. He had his whole life ahead of him.

Somehow, as the sirens loomed in the distance and blood continued to pool around us, I knew God was not listening to me. It turned out that Louis *had* accomplished what he was supposed to do on this earth; I just didn't know it then.

It was at that moment that I knew my world had disappeared, and that my life, as I knew it, was no longer my own. Somewhere in the back of my mind, I heard someone say, "Welcome to my world. Welcome to hell," as I slipped into a sea of darkness from which I knew there would be no return. The voice was only partly right.

11

Descent into Darkness

"My heart sobs with uncontrollable grief;
I search for answers, but find no relief.
The skies have darkened, no longer bright,
for my child is gone forever from sight."

—*Unknown*

Somehow I was able to call my parents using my cell phone and let them know what was happening. Still in shock, I gave someone the keys to my car and asked him to put it in his driveway, as I was not able to drive and would be going to the hospital in the ambulance with my son.

Almost as an afterthought, I grabbed my workout bag from the backseat of my car and waited for the paramedics to put Louis in the ambulance. As the EMTs rolled Louis over using cervical spine precautions, he was catatonic and in respiratory arrest, and they heard a gurgling noise.

The paramedics intubated him, and Lou was taken by ambulance to the awaiting helicopter. As we pulled into the emergency parking lot, I saw nurses and doctors standing outside with a stretcher.

The ambulance driver slowed down, shook his head, and then proceeded to the Life Flight helicopter pad that was waiting to transport my son to the University of Massachusetts Medical Center in Worcester.

My Uncle Joe, who had been at my mother's house when she had gotten the call, knew how serious it was. He said he had heard the helicopter as he was walking in the door. He had actually just buried his own sister that morning, but pushed his grief aside and left to meet me at the hospital to offer his unconditional support.

As I got out of the ambulance, the attendants proceeded to transfer Louis into the helicopter. If anyone was a welcome sight at that moment, it was Uncle Joe. I had been alone for almost an hour with Louis, trying to comprehend what had happened, trying to deal with the unimaginable, and feeling so totally helpless that I fell into his arms, crying. Once again, it was an act of human kindness I will always remember.

A police officer approached us and told me that they were flying Louis to UMass Medical. I told him there was no way they were taking my son without me. I couldn't drive, and I needed to be with him from that moment on, not an hour later when someone would be able to drive me and God knows what might have happened.

The officer looked at me with pity in his eyes and said he'd be right back. As I watched him anxiously, he talked with the pilot, and then waved me over. I didn't know at the time that civilians were never allowed to ride in the helicopter, but maybe the look on my face and the severity of the accident made the rules a moot point. In any event, I was allowed to accompany my son to the hospital.

As we left the ground, I was never as thankful in my entire life as I was for the kindness and sympathy this man had shown. Thanks to his selfless act of generosity, I would not lose a minute of precious time with my son. The flight took less than fifteen minutes, and as we landed on the helicopter port at the hospital, there were already doctors and nurses waiting with a stretcher to take him directly into surgery.

Meanwhile, I was led to a waiting room and was told the nurse would bring me information about the extent of my son's injuries as soon as he was out of surgery. As I sat on the couch in my own private room, cell phone in one hand, my workout bag containing a change of clothes in the other, I saw nothing and felt nothing. It was a sense of numbness like I'd never experienced, a pre-death as still as night that left me a vacant shell, in mental hibernation until the other shoe dropped.

All the while, I watched nurses, doctors, and various people walking by, looking at me with questions in their eyes. I looked at the wallpaper, the chairs, the floor, anywhere but into their eyes, and waited. After what felt like an eternity, a doctor finally came into the room. I knew immediately that I didn't want to hear what he had to say. His eyes were too kind and too sympathetic. I knew that he must have children and was perhaps putting himself in my shoes. Although I dreaded hearing them, the words that I heard next brought me back to reality. My son had suffered massive brain damage, he was breathing with the help of a respirator, and while doctors were still working on him, the prognosis was bleak.

As I tried to comprehend what I had just heard, I looked at the doctor and begged him, "Please save my baby! Please!" The tears started running down my face as the doctor said they were doing the best they could and that he would return when he had more information. I trusted this man implicitly, and his eyes told me he was telling the truth, even as they held out little hope.

A little while later, a nurse came in and told me to use the phone in the office if I needed to call anyone. I called Tony and explained what had happened, and he immediately left to come to the hospital. By now, other family members were starting to filter into the waiting room—my sisters and their husbands, my brother and sister-in-law, uncles, aunts—soon the room I'd occupied alone was filled with those near and dear to my heart. As each one came in, I looked at them, repeated what the doctor had told me, and then went quickly back to nowhere, staring at the floor and the walls, waiting for Tony, waiting for the doctor to come back and tell me Louis was fine, waiting, I suppose, for the inevitable.

A nurse finally came back to tell me Louis was out of surgery and was being moved to the head-trauma floor. That didn't sound promising. She explained that now we would be able to go up to that floor, where there was another waiting room, and we'd be closer to him. My first thought was: *A waiting room for what?* As I looked at the nurse, waiting for more information, she said, "The doctor will be up to see you soon."

Thankfully, Tony arrived just as we had settled into yet another room. He couldn't believe what had happened and he, too, was in shock. His bereft eyes mirrored what I was thinking: *Things like this just don't happen to people you know, let alone your own son.*

The wait seemed endless. Although I was too upset to handle it myself, I somehow had the forethought to have my sister call my friend and co-worker, Stephanie, to tell her what had happened and not to expect me back at work. I held onto the bracelet Louis had given me seven years ago, and prayed. The doctor finally came in. I held onto the chair, knowing what I was going to hear, begging God to let me be wrong. Louis had suffered severe brain damage and was being kept alive on life support. They had done everything they could to relieve the pressure on his brain, and when that didn't work, he had been declared legally dead. "However," the doctor offered, "a small portion of his brain is still alive."

I stared at the doctor and said, "Miracles do happen. If a small portion of his brain is alive, then he'll recover."

The doctor looked at me as I'm sure he had to hundreds of other mothers who weren't willing to accept the fact their child was brain-dead. He said very softly,

"Yes, miracles *do* happen, but not in this case." Then the words came out that I refused to hear: "Your son would be a vegetable if he survived."

As I tried to absorb what the doctor was saying, I thought that if I could just go back in time and pick him up earlier, then as we pulled in the driveway and the time came for him to leave this earth, I would be able to stop him before he left, because he would be home safe and sound. Yes, that was it. *God, please take me back in time, just this once. I promise I'll never ask you for anything again.* But God wasn't listening to me that night. He was with Louis.

The nurse finally came back and told me that I could go and see my son. As I followed her down the seemingly endless hall, the longest one I would ever walk, I forced a smile on my face for my son's sake, and walked into his hospital room, head held high despite the crushing grief that already threatened to suck me down forever.

As I walked into the trauma area, the nurse looked at me and said by way of a warning, "He may look a little bloated, because we have him on intravenous liquids, and you can also expect some cuts and bruises." His bed was next to the window, and as I followed the nurse, all I could hear was the beeping of heart monitors everywhere.

As I walked over to my son's bed, not knowing what to expect, my heart was beating so fast that I couldn't catch my breath. Then I saw him and suddenly felt calmer. Yes, he was swollen. He was on a heart monitor and a respirator, and life support was actually breathing for him, but the bruises were surprisingly minor. To me, he was the most beautiful boy in the world. He looked so peaceful lying there: just like he was sleeping.

I went over, sat by his side, and held his hand, still warm with blood and life. How could a hand that warm, a face that peaceful, be considered legally dead? I stared at him for a long time, not knowing if he even knew I was there.

I sat by the window, kissed him, and told him how much I loved him. Maybe he heard me; maybe he didn't. I wanted to think that he did, but he was in a coma. It was the worst moment of my life.

Just the day before, we had been shopping at the mall; tonight, he lay there on life support. How could this have happened? I couldn't imagine him not being in my life. Children aren't supposed to die before their parents. As the past started running through my mind, I thought of all the wonderful and happy times we had shared.

I knew my son would not be with me for much longer, and I had to accept it. But I couldn't and I wouldn't. My family came in, one by one, and Tony came in to take his seat next to me. As long as there was some part of his brain that remained alive, there was a chance.

Nurses and aids came and went, washing his face, removing the blood from the cuts he had sustained, bringing in warm blankets, and offering some kind of conversation, but I just sat there talking to Louis, holding his hand and secretly willing him to open his eyes and say, "Hi, Mom. Don't worry; I'm going to be fine." But he never did.

My ex-husband had arrived a few hours after we got to the hospital, and he sat with Louis with a blanket around him because he was cold. Finally, around midnight, he asked the nurse if there was anywhere he could sleep, because he was tired. The nurse sent him up to another floor, and that's where he spent the next seven hours.

Sometime during the night, a doctor asked me to come down the hall to his office. Once I was there, he asked me to consider organ donation. He explained the procedure as delicately as he could, but I told him it wasn't a good time for me. I needed to get back to my son's bedside; I couldn't waste time sitting in his office. He understood, and I left.

When I returned to Louis's bedside, I held his hand in mine and kissed him, and all I could think about was what had just been asked of me. I was being forced to accept my son's death at a time when I still held onto hope. And yet, as memories flooded my mind of times he had asked me for money for homeless people we had walked by in Boston; of his love of children, always hugging and playing with them; of the tears he had shed when he knew he had hurt me through his mistakes; I knew in my heart it was what Louis would have wanted. And who knew him better than me?

I went back to the doctor's office and told him I had made the decision to donate his organs. My family and Tony agreed that Louis would have wanted to save as many lives as he could. So the nurse came in and took fifty vials of blood from him, then they gave him four transfusions to put the blood back into his body. They immediately started faxing information out to all surrounding hospitals to match organ recipients.

They had people ready in hospitals, waiting for transplants. When my ex-husband came down from his night of sleeping, he looked at me and said, "How long is this going to last?"

Appalled at the ignorance of his remark, I informed him what I had decided while he had been sleeping and told him that we would be going into a conference room to sign the necessary papers. He said nothing.

Once we went into the room, I signed the papers and gave them to him. He looked at everyone and said, "I can't sign this; I don't want my son cut up."

The room was quiet. I said, "Do you know how many lives Louis could save? Don't you get it? He would have wanted this."

My ex-husband just said, "I don't care." I asked the doctors if they could get a court order allowing this procedure with my signature alone, but the doctors said both parents had to sign. His disregard for saving other lives was beyond my comprehension, but again, his reaction was far from surprising. So I made the decision to become a donor myself and at least save the lives that Louis had not been able to.

I went out once to talk to his friends. They had found out about the accident and were sitting in the hallway, clumped together, as if seeking comfort from one another. As I walked out, Brett was the first one I saw. As I hugged him, we both cried for what we knew were Lou's final hours.

My family tried to comfort me, not knowing what to say or how to say it. In our discomfort, words remained unspoken. Just as silently I went back to sit by my son's side, and waited. I continued to wash away the trickles of blood from his eyes and nose, realizing that this meant more pressure was building up on his brain. I had experienced death before, but nothing had prepared me for this.

The doctors took Louis back down to surgery a few more times, if only to relieve the constant pressure on his brain. During those few times, I would go in the waiting room and lay on the couch, waiting for my son to come back to his room so I could go back in. My family was still there, some sleeping, some talking, some just staring, as I had done only hours before.

Tony took me down to the chapel in the hospital, and as I stood outside the door, knowing I couldn't go in, he urged me just to sit for a few minutes, away from everything else. I finally sat in the last pew in the back, as if that somehow proved that I didn't want to be there. How could I pray for something I knew was never going to happen, and, more importantly, why would I?

I was angry at God. He was taking away my son, my soul mate, my life. I turned to Tony and said, "I've been through a lot over the years and survived, but I will never survive the loss of Louis—never." And somehow, he knew. He knew how both our lives would change forever and that the loss of my son would isolate my love for him for many years to come.

We eventually went back to the waiting room. It was now 2:00 AM Family members started to leave, saying they would be back in a few hours. Everyone was exhausted, both mentally and physically. My sisters took my mother home so she could get some rest. But both my brothers-in-law, Kevin and Jamey, stayed throughout the night, keeping vigil with me. Few words were ever spoken, but in my heart I couldn't have felt more love for them than I did that night.

Sometime during the early hours of the morning, I saw Lou's stomach move, just slightly, but he looked like he was breathing. I told Tony to look at him, but the movement had been so slight that he hadn't noticed it. Eventually it started becoming more pronounced, almost like he was gasping for air.

I immediately called for the nurse. Once she arrived, I showed her what I hoped was my miracle. She took all his vital signs, checked the monitor and ventilator, and shook her head. He was still hanging on, but so slightly that it made no difference. The nurse would let the doctors know, but it was probably some type of nerve reaction. I slumped back in my chair, totally defeated, and cried for my son, for my loss, and for a life cut so tragically short.

Suddenly, something made me turn my head and look toward the window. At that moment it was 6:45 AM. As I looked outside, wondering what had pulled me so strongly in that direction, I saw the beginning of the sunrise. I couldn't turn my head away. Tony was also watching. We watched the dark gray clouds part, and beams of sunlight pushed past them to rise and begin a new day. Despite the grim circumstances, it was the most beautiful sunrise I had ever seen.

And as we watched, I felt the presence of my son so strongly and so absolutely that I felt paralyzed, and I knew that he had gone at that very moment. He was tired of this life—wanting to stay, but needing to go home. My son had stayed long enough to help me through the past two days, maybe to help me adjust, to help me in some way to deal with the worst nightmare a mother can suffer, and perhaps to prepare me for what lay ahead. He knew I had needed this time next to him to grieve and prepare. Even in death, his love for me had shown through. As tears fell from my eyes, I heard, somewhere in the distance, "I love you way past Jesus."

What I didn't know then was that my sister Gloria was up at the same time, changing her clothes before returning to the hospital, and that she felt the very same feeling when she saw the sunrise that morning.

I turned my head back and looked at Tony. I looked at my son, with his hand still in mine, and I didn't say a word. The doctors came in to take Louis back down to surgery. Tony left for a quick meeting at work, but he would be back. Both my brothers-in-law left to go to their jobs, and my twin brought my mother back with her.

Silently, my mother and I waited for Louis to return. When he did, there were three doctors with him. One of the surgeons came over to me and said, "I've never seen someone hang on so desperately with such severe head injuries, but we have done everything we can do and the decision of whether to shut off the life support has to be made. What is the decision?"

They told me I could keep him on life support, in which case he would be sent to a rest home to live out his life as a vegetable, completely brain dead; or they could shut off the life support and let him go. A sudden feeling of selfishness settled in my mind. If I kept him on life support, at least I could still have him, visit with him, and hold him, and he wouldn't *really* be dead.

On the other hand, my unselfish feeling told me it was time to let him go. As much as I loved my son, how could I keep him on life support just to satisfy my own needs? I remember a male nurse that was on duty that morning who came over, talked to me, made sure Louis had clean sheets and blankets, and asked me if I needed some coffee. He was so sensitive and caring. I remember asking him if he had seen Lou's tattoo that said MOM on his leg. He smiled and said, "He must love you very much to have done that."

Why I asked him that, I don't know. Was I just making sure he knew how much my son loved me? I was running on pure impulse at that point, and not everything made sense, but it lives in my memory to this day: images, fragments, and comments, burned into my mind forever.

I was very tired, so I put my head on the bed, held Lou's hand, and just rested. He was given the last rites twice during his final eighteen hours. Then the final moment came. The doctors asked me if I had made a decision, and, looking at my mother for support, I finally said, "Yes, shut off the life support."

It was 2:15 PM on November 24, 1998. The nurse came over and turned the volume down on the heart monitor. As they shut off the life support, we waited, still hoping for a miracle. At 2:45, the nurse came over to me and said simply, "He's gone."

For the second time that day, I felt my soul being ripped out of my body. He had left this earth at sunrise, I was as sure of that as I was of my own name. Tony, Gloria, and I had all felt him leave—he had let us know he was leaving—but now there was no doubt in anyone's mind that he had died.

I let go of his hand and kissed him, and the nurses gave me his chain with the cross on it and his diamond earring that I had bought him years before. As I stared at them in my trembling hands, I realized I had broken a promise to him. I had promised to protect and shield him from all sorrow and pain, encourage him when hope had diminished, and love him unconditionally from the moment he had been placed in my arms, never thinking that the one thing I would never be able to protect him from was death.

As I left the hospital with my sisters and mother on that fateful day, I climbed into the backseat, wanting to be alone to grieve by myself. There was nothing anyone could say. Fortunately, my family knew this, and the typical "I know how you must feel," "It was his time," and "I'm so sorry" were never spoken. We grieved in our own ways: silently; alone.

My grief was, to say the least, unbearable. In the hours that followed, loneliness and emptiness set in, and I lost all perception of time. I had lost my future, my second chance, but most of all I had lost someone who had loved me beyond belief. I had failed to protect him from death, and in return, I had lost my very soul.

Deep down, I knew the worst was yet to come, but I didn't care anymore. I had been given the wrong dream and had lived it. I knew I would never be the same person again, and what I did become was nothing short of my ongoing nightmares. I would live a life of self-destruction for the next five years, until one day my son would show me once again how much he loved me, and I would finally return from darkness to light.

When I got home that day, family and friends immediately started coming over and offering support and condolences, and asking questions that couldn't be answered. They answered the telephone as it began ringing off the hook, while I went into my room, lie down on my bed, and simply let the tears flow.

I needed to be alone in my grief, and my family somehow knew it. Tony arrived with his clothes, so he could stay with me, and someone ordered food, but most important to me was their presence throughout the afternoon and night. I would have to go to the funeral parlor in the morning to pick out a casket—something, if given the choice, I would have let my family do, but it was my responsibility. I was on my own and knew I didn't want anyone else to have to make that kind of decision for me. It was too personal, and I wanted everything just perfect for my son.

After everyone had left, Tony and I went to bed. I knew I wouldn't be able to sleep once I put my head down. I had been up for more than forty-eight hours, and was mentally and physically exhausted. The minute I closed my eyes, I relived the accident, the hospital, and my son's death all over again. Sadly, these were nightmares I knew I would have for the rest of my life. I finally got out of bed and went into Louis's room and slept in his bed. Suddenly, I needed to be close to him. His favorite yellow blanket from childhood and his favorite stuffed animals were still on his bed. He had always loved Garfield when he was young, and I had bought him Garfield sheets and pillowcases, which were now on the bed.

Sometime that night, in another town, my brother-in-law Kevin, who had stayed by Lou's bedside all night, took his dog out for his nightly walk in the woods. As he sat on a rock with the dog, also trying to comprehend what had happened, the dog started a low growl, the wind seemed to stop, and everything was still. Kevin didn't remember if he saw or just heard Louis telling him to tell me how much he loved me and that he was all right. It was a feeling he had never experienced and could not explain it any other way.

I often wondered why my son had chosen to speak to Kevin and not one of his friends, but years later, I realized that I probably wouldn't have believed his friends, knowing the extent of their grief. Louis had sent Kevin that message because he knew I would believe him.

The next morning, I somehow got out of bed. I was alone again, because Tony had to get back to work. I looked in the mirror and stared at the image before me, not quite believing what I saw. My eyes were red and puffy from lack of sleep, as well as from the endless tears and the horrific nightmares that had plagued me all night. I looked like I had aged and was wearing someone else's years-older face. It definitely was not the face I had looked at a mere two days ago.

Somewhere, the phone was ringing. I didn't want to answer it. I didn't want to talk to anyone, but still I picked it up. My mother was on the phone, asking if I was okay and reminding me that we needed to go to the funeral home. My hands were shaking, my mind was somewhere else, and all the while, I felt I was talking too much. She said she would be over to pick me up in a few hours.

My twin also came with us. When you have a twin, whether you're identical or fraternal, your feelings are closer than those of another type of sibling. We had always felt each other's pain more deeply than other people. She had stayed with me when Charlie had been killed, and now she was with me when Louis died. She felt my pain as deeply as I did, and I hope she knew her presence in those dark, dreary days brought much comfort to me.

We arrived at the funeral parlor and walked through the door. Although I tried to control myself, my tears were uncontrollable. I didn't want to be here picking out a casket that I thought Louis would like. I didn't want to talk with David, the funeral director. But in the end, I did these things, with the help of my mother and sister. It turned out that David was sensitive, caring, and understanding and only asked what he absolutely had to. Even though this was his business, even though he did this with grieving families every day, I felt he was more caring and sensitive than usual, knowing what I was going through.

His job wasn't easy. I simply couldn't talk without crying. I couldn't even remember the littlest details he was asking me. My short-term memory was suddenly and inexplicably gone. I looked to my mother and Mike to fill in what I couldn't. An autopsy was being performed on my son, so David would not be able to pick up his body until Wednesday, the day before Thanksgiving, which meant the wake would take place on Friday, with the funeral to follow on Saturday morning, November 28.

Once the details of the wake and funeral were over, we left to go home. My mother always had a big Thanksgiving dinner for our extended family. This year, for the first time in as long as I could remember, we would have dinner for just the immediate family. It mattered little to me; all I wanted to do was to go to bed and never get up. I had no appetite; my stomach was a nervous wreck, while the rest of me felt like someone was reaching in and twisting every nerve in my body. I went through the next two days in a fog, though somehow I managed to pick out the clothes I wanted Louis to be buried in: his favorite red sweater and dungarees. Suits were neither in his vocabulary nor in his closet. One certainly wasn't going to be in his casket.

The wake was to be held from four until eight. As I dressed and put on some makeup, my sisters came over to check on me. Although I told them I was fine, my twin said, "You need to put something around your eyes; they're so swollen." I tried putting on more makeup, but that made it worse. My "keep your head up and smile" face had disappeared, but I did want to attempt to look good. I don't know why; maybe I thought I'd get less sympathy and no one would see me crying.

I had been so tough throughout the years that it was extremely difficult to break down and act the way I really felt. But I simply couldn't help it; my mind and body were rebelling against me at the same time, and I simply couldn't hold up to the one-two punch. Mike said, "Do you have any Preparation H in the bathroom?" I told her I didn't know, but she went in and found some. Horrified as I was at the thought of putting it on my face, I did, because by this time, my eyes were actually tiny slits. Amazingly, it worked well enough to at least take some of the swelling away.

At long last, Tony drove us to the funeral home. As I got out, I felt weak, nauseous, and light-headed, and my stomach felt like someone had punched it. I walked through the door with my family behind me, and David immediately came to my side, put his hand under my elbow, and brought me to the casket. I felt like a walking zombie. As I stood in front of the casket looking at my beautiful son, the tears I tried to stop fell like rain. I was sobbing so hard that I couldn't breathe. The depth of my grief was unbearable. It was the deepest pain I had ever felt in my life.

As I looked around at all the beautiful flowers and pictures of Louis that David had placed so carefully around the room, I wanted to die at that very moment. Little did I know that this would be a wish that would last for a very long time. I had decided to have an open casket. As his mother, I thought Lou looked beautiful and peaceful. However, the rest of my family saw what I couldn't: because of the massive head injuries, Louis didn't look quite like himself. After asking Tony's opinion, I closed the casket.

As people started to come in, everything became a blur to me. Many thoughtful, caring words were spoken; many embraces I needed desperately were given; and many friends from years gone by showed up. It was almost too overwhelming for me. The night was cold, but people lined up outside and down the sidewalk to come inside.

The visiting hours were supposed to end at eight, but when the time came, David walked up to me and said that there were still so many people waiting outside that he would wait until everyone had come in and paid their respects. He was one of the most professional and caring people I had ever met, and it moved me to tears to know there were people in this world like him. He truly felt my pain, and responded in kind. We had known each other before only well enough to say hi, but after this, I would always remember him as the person who held us all together. Three hundred people attended the visitation that night, and finally, at around 10:00 PM, we were ready to go home. Friends from the telephone company had made arrangements to send over cold-cut platters and antipasto, so we invited family, friends, and even David to come over.

The day of the funeral was bright and sunny, and not as cold as the day before. I said my final good-bye to my son in private after everyone had left for church. David opened the casket, and I put a picture of the two of us in happier times inside, held and kissed him one final time, then, without a backward glance, left for church. As hard as it was to say good-bye, I simply couldn't bear to drag the torment out any longer.

A girlfriend I had worked with way back in the early seventies drove down from New Hampshire to attend the funeral. We had lost touch over the years, and seeing her was wonderful. I couldn't believe a friend from twenty years ago still remembered us. She sent me a beautiful letter shortly after the funeral, writing: "As I drove to Louis's funeral this morning, the sky was alive with low, dark clouds and a bright sun above it all, shining its rays through the clouds. I couldn't help thinking that it was a welcoming home for your son. It was a profound moment."

I couldn't believe it: there was that sunrise again—the sunrise when I held my son that very first morning of his life, the sunrise of his death, and now the sunrise on the morning I would bury him. I saved her letter, not just because she was my friend, but for what those words meant to me.

It was a beautiful mass. At one point, a friend of mine sang "Through the Years" by Kenny Rogers, because Louis had told me one day that he wanted that song for his wedding when we danced the mother-and-son dance. As I listened to the song, I cried for my loss, for my soul, for my son, and for a dance that would never be.

As we stood up to leave for the cemetery, I felt Tony holding my elbow very tightly. During mass, I had almost fainted, but I had pulled myself together to make that final walk with my son, to lay him to rest in peace.

Crucial Correspondence

This letter was written by Nicole Stetson, Lou's girlfriend for six years She was the love of his life and now was the daughter I never had. I chose to include this letter because she was the only girl he dated that he truly loved. How do I know? Because he told me!

Dear Louis,

I can see you holding the steering wheel in that way that I always thought was cute, looking at me and smiling and holding my hand. Your touch would send butterflies into my stomach. I loved that feeling of just love. To look in your eyes, you didn't have to know you to see who you were. The loyalty you felt toward your friends and family showed in the way you looked at everyone you met.

There are so many songs that remind me of you and what could have been. No one has ever looked at me the way you did; you loved me for every dorky thing about me. I regret not following my heart; I knew I loved you and that if I was to ask, you would have given me everything, but I wasn't ready; you still were at a place in your life when alcohol played a big part in it, and I distanced myself from you because of it.

I regret that more than words could say, because I can still see the look on your face the last time I saw you, when in your eyes I could see that you just needed someone, me, to be there for you. I tell myself that I was young and wasn't ready, because I shouldn't feel guilty for you dying, but I do and I always will. When I hear "Touch Me" by the Doors, I remember you said that song reminded you of us: "I'm going to love you until the stars fall from the sky for you and I..." and it's ironic that that will be the only time we will meet again.

Your memory is starting to fade as I move on with my life, but even as I cannot remember every time I saw you or everything that was said, the feeling is still in the pit of my stomach, just an ache to be with you again. I miss you, Lou, your smile and your big heart and the love you have for your mother that would turn off most girls but was a quality I found to show how much you love and give of yourself. I say "is" and "love you have," because I know you are still with us and supporting the people you love, because that's what you did when you were here with us, and there is no way you could see any of the people you cared about hurting. I counted on that support during very hard moments in my life and still will for my future.

There is never a day that I don't think of you, or that something doesn't remind me of you. Please know that I loved you for you and what I saw in your eyes and that if life had dealt us a different hand, I would have given you everything I am. But also know that a big part of who I am now is because of your life and going through the pain of your death.

12

The Long Journey Home

"Sometime in your life you will go on a journey.
It will be the longest journey you have ever taken.
It is the journey to find yourself."

—*Katherine Sharp*

The days and weeks following the funeral, I have to admit, were just a fog to me. Nothing could have prepared me for something like this. I had nightmares when I went to bed. I would toss and turn the entire night. I would open my eyes in the morning wondering where Louis was, waiting to hear the sounds of his radio in the next room, and waiting for him to ask me to cook breakfast—all sounds I would never hear again.

Guilt encompassed every waking minute of the day—what if I had been home earlier, what if I hadn't worked out so long—all the "what ifs" that would forever remain unanswered. I had not been able to drive since the accident. I was afraid to get behind the wheel of the car, so my family drove me everywhere I needed to go.

The grief was intense and disabling, consuming every waking minute of my day. I felt totally disorganized and confused. My son's death had robbed me of the person I used to be. I would have to adjust to this person I was now, someone I didn't know. I was in a totally different place in my life, and it was a place where I didn't want to be.

His death was so traumatic that it was beyond description. My feelings could not be put into words. Words could not describe the depth of devastation I felt. How was I going to get through the days, weeks, and years that would follow? Was this going to be my life forever? Never moving on, unable to drive, unable to sleep? I thought of all the people throughout the ages who'd lost loved ones, and wondered how they'd gotten through it. The thoughts didn't last long. There was only me, only Louis. That was all that had mattered. Now he was gone.

My rage was overwhelming, and I had no one to turn to. My family grieved for their grandchild, nephew, and cousin; feelings that were almost—*almost*—as devastating as mine. I truly felt at times that I would go insane. When family, friends, and co-workers asked how I was doing, my response was always the same: "Fine." How could I explain the constant, unrelenting pain that was buried deep inside of me? It was a feeling I would not be able to escape for years.

I had picked out a double plot at the cemetery. "Two for the price of one," as the ad said. The spot was beautiful, and the setting was serene and peaceful: it was in front of the woods, with a small stream off to the side. It was a place I knew Louis would have liked, and one day I would join him in the same spot. The headstone I had chosen was unusual; it was one of the newer colors, a color that would stand out from the others.

It's strange how the mind works when a tragedy occurs: you're still thinking of your loved one and what they would want, as if they knew or even cared at that point. An ocean scene with two Adirondack chairs sitting in the sand was engraved on the front of the stone, with a picture of the two of us together. It was our favorite place—one that would only be a distant memory now.

It was hardest for me to recall the words Louis had spoken on our last visit to the beach. He had promised to buy me that house, with only two chairs, for just the two of us. Now the closest we would get to that place was when I came to visit this headstone.

I finally spoke with the police about the accident. They had been kind enough to wait a few weeks before asking me for a statement. Here I was once again, a witness to another accident, another death: my son's. The state police had decided to press charges against the boy who had killed Louis.

The driver of the car, who was the same age as Louis, had been driving home and dropped something on the floor. He'd had his left hand on the steering wheel, turning as he tried to pick the object up, and had ended up hitting Louis as a result. He went into shock, and it was a few minutes before he got out of the car and ran over to me, hysterical, crying, still a young boy himself, not knowing what to do, seeking help from the only mother he could find—the mother, it just so happened, of his dying victim.

By then, a paramedic who had been driving behind him, as well as other witnesses on the scene had stopped. What had been my final moment alone with my son had become a desperate attempt to stop his bleeding and get him to the hospital. I couldn't focus on the driver of the car; I just wanted him far away from me. As the police began talking to other witnesses, they asked him to stay away from the scene. As I glanced over at him, I knew my nightmare would soon be his also—a nightmare we would both live with for the rest of our lives, only on different levels.

Condolence cards, floral arrangements, and mass intentions arrived every day. Jack had sent a beautiful arrangement of flowers to my house, along with a card reading: "Pat, I realize no words or flowers can undo your unthinkable tragedy. I only hope you can find some comfort in the knowledge that friends from all over the country are thinking of you. Love, Jack."

It was from my best friend in the world. Pat, Mike and Jack—so long ago, yet seeming like yesterday, we had pledged that our friendship would last forever. And, amazingly, it had. Friends at the telephone company had donated money for food after the funeral, had sent beautiful flowers to the funeral parlor, and called constantly to offer whatever they could to lessen the pain.

As I read through the cards one morning after that first week, I quickly realized that some were from friends I had worked with more than twenty years ago. Again, those bonds we had formed so many years ago were suddenly returning, letting me know that my friends were still there during my grief.

One day, as I picked up my mail, I noticed a card with familiar handwriting and knew instantly who it was from. So many years had gone by, yet he still had remembered, and with a card filled with concern and sympathy for the loss of my son. As I held the card, I was able to reach down to that hidden place where I had put him a lifetime ago and I knew he was still there and always would be. It brought tears to my eyes, but it also brought a smile to my face that for one brief moment actually felt real—a smile of long ago.

My days would begin with such a feeling of loss and severe grief in the morning that I'd just want to close my eyes again, if only so I wouldn't have to wake up. I'd wander through the house, completely exhausted, with eyes that remained constantly swollen and red from crying. Chronic fatigue and exhaustion became an everyday occurrence; I wondered how I had ever had the energy to work, drive, talk, plan…or live.

An overwhelming feeling of complete emptiness engulfed every minute of every day. I longed to hold my son. I promised God that if I could just see and hug him one last time, I'd never ask for anything again. God continued to ignore me.

It became such an effort to take a shower and wash my hair that days would go by without my doing either one. The minute I got up, I couldn't wait for the day to end so I could go back to bed and hopefully sleep as long as I could, just to forget. I had no appetite, and when I did eat, I would be sick to my stomach and run for the bathroom the minute I quit chewing. So I stopped eating, and instead lived on coffee and bottled water. By the time my birthday arrived on the day after Christmas, I weighed ninety pounds.

My friends from work came over just before Christmas with presents and Chinese food. As we talked, I attempted to eat, pretending it was great and not wanting to hurt their feelings as they kept filling my plate. I didn't know it then, but they were horrified at what they saw had happened in a matter of only four weeks. As for myself, I was horrified by what I saw reflected in their eyes: I saw concern, sympathy, and helplessness in their faces. They wanted to help erase my pain in any way possible, but just didn't know how.

Denial cushioned my mind; the loss was so horrible that I simply couldn't face it. All the years of being strong and tough, of training myself never to show my weakness or show my real feelings, crumbled into a thousand pieces around me. I was under a doctor's care, and returning to work was simply not an option for me.

Time stood still once more. There were no more tomorrows, just an endless, insufferable today for the rest of my life. I lived not from day to day, but from minute to minute. My days began and ended the same as the day before, with the heart-wrenching pain only a parent feels with the loss of a child. When I looked in the mirror, a face would stare back at me, so haunting, so incredibly sad and broken that I began avoiding any mirror I passed by. Along with the psychological changes that were occurring, there were physiological ones as well. At forty-six years old, I went through menopause, which sometimes happens with an older woman when her body undergoes a traumatic experience.

One afternoon shortly after the funeral, I was standing in my kitchen, talking with Tony. My arms were resting on the counter, and all of a sudden the bracelet Louis had bought me seven years ago fell off. There was no reason for it. I hadn't been doing anything except talking. I stared at the bracelet lying on the counter.

Tony said, "How did that happen?" But it was more of a statement than a question because he didn't believe what he had just seen. I had never taken the bracelet off in all that time, because it gave me a feeling of closeness to my son that I desperately needed. Was Louis telling me to let go? Feebly, I brought it over to Tony, and as he put it back on, I started to cry. Wasn't it bad enough that he had died? Did he now want me to take the bracelet off too? There must have been another reason. There had to be; I was sure of it, but I didn't know what it was.

The next night, as I was sleeping, I dreamed that someone was holding my hand with such love that I felt it throughout my entire body. Still drowsy from lack of sleep, I felt as though I was awake, but I just wasn't sure. When I woke up the next morning, I lay in bed trying to remember what had happened, and once again the same feeling of love and warmth was there surrounding me. It had been my son holding my hand. No one else could have made me feel that much love at that moment in my life. He needed me to know he was still with me—if not physically, at least deep in my heart, where he belonged. For just the briefest moment, I went back in time to the days when he would wake up from one of his nightmares and I would go into his room, hold his hand, hug him, and reassure him everything was going to be all right. Then I cried for those feelings I'd never have again, but also because of what my son had just given me: hope—hope that maybe someday life might be a little better; hope that some love inside me had still survived. It was enough, I suppose, to nourish what was left of my heart.

From that day on, my son remained with me. I felt his presence around me and in my heart. It was a feeling I couldn't begin to describe, but I knew he would stay with me until it was time to leave, until I was strong enough to let him go, and I clung to that feeling for years.

Every day set me on a journey I wanted to forget. Nightmares of the accident crept out of my dreams and followed me into daylight; eventually they started to intrude into my daily life. I would have flashbacks when I least expected them. I would relive his death, the hospital room, and the wake. Every moment seemed like it was right there and real, and I was made to relive it all over again. Tony would come over at night and help me as much as he could, but I was a total mess, and he watched helplessly as I descended into a world of darkness—a world he wanted no part of; a world he was stuck in.

One day, my mother asked if I would go to see our local priest. He was a wonderful man, and he'd had Louis in catechism since the fourth grade. My mother was a devout Catholic who went to church every Sunday. My family didn't know what else to do. They offered comfort and support; they offered anything I needed, but they knew nothing was working.

I just wanted to stay in my own world. How could I talk about what I was feeling, when they had never experienced it themselves? They knew I was hurting very deeply. I was in a severe depression and missing my son terribly. So, to make my mother happy, I agreed to go. He was the last person I wanted to talk to and the church was the last place I wanted to be. I was so angry that God had taken my son from me. I had finally started to drive a little, but every time I got behind the wheel, my stomach turned.

It did so now. I was nervous, and drove so slowly that people would pass me, but I just couldn't help it. I knew what a car could do if someone ran out in front of me. As I drove down the street and pulled into the parking lot of the church, I asked myself again what I was doing there. I had wanted to make my mother happy, but deep down; I knew I didn't want to be there.

Grimly determined to get through this and get back home as soon as possible, I walked up the stairs and rang the bell. I figured that since I was here, I might as well ask the person closest to God why this had happened. As I sat in the living room, the priest walked in. I immediately started crying. Something I simply couldn't control anymore had washed over me at his very presence, and I was powerless to prevent it.

He shook my hand, asked me how I was doing (he didn't want to know how I was really feeling), and then sat down in the chair. He saw the bitterness, hurt, and pain in my eyes, and if the saying "The eyes are the mirror to the soul" was true; it couldn't have been more accurate. I asked all the questions I needed, but he had no answers. I didn't want to be there, and he knew it.

He looked at me and said, "The day of the funeral, as I walked up to the pulpit, I looked down at the paper I had written about Louis the night before. As I started reading, I felt something strange come over me, as if someone was forcing me to look at the people." He looked at me to make sure I was listening, and then said, "I pushed the paper aside and spoke of the boy I had known over the years, of the man he had become, and of the senseless tragedy of a young life cut short."

I asked him what had happened, and the priest replied, "I don't know, Pat. It was almost as if Louis didn't want me to read about his life from a piece of paper, but to talk about him as I really knew him." Once again, here was a message from my son, only this time it was a message to a priest who had also been his friend.

I told him how angry I was with God, and he shook his head and said, "There is always a reason why God does things." *But,* I thought, *how could that be?* Whatever that reason was, it made no sense to me. Why would he take away the only thing in the world I loved so much? There would never be an answer I would understand; not now; not ever.

Finally, the question I had longed to ask leapt from my lips: "Father, why did God let me see my son's death?"

The priest said, "Pat, everyone knows how close you were to Louis. It's a small town. Louis called you four times that night. You were the first one he saw when he came into this world; maybe he wanted you to be the last one he saw as he left this earth."

These were words I would remember the rest of my life—words that made sense to me. Louis knew that if I had received a phone call from the hospital I would not have been able to understand his death. At least this gave me hope. Even if Louis didn't know he was going to die, God did and gave me that time with him.

Louis had touched a lot of lives when he died, and, in his own inimitable way, had left messages that I would one day receive from the people he knew I would believe. Only the ones he talked with know this is possible. Other people refused to believe. But that was fine with me. The ones he chose were the ones he trusted. Should it surprise me that God was at the top of his list?

1999

Three months after Louis died; I felt I needed to go back to work. I discussed this with my doctor, and, after much hesitation, she decided that I could work half-days, but she was still not comfortable letting me go back to full-time work. Reluctantly, I agreed.

My first day back proved to be exactly what I needed. It was great to be back to some kind of normalcy. Everyone was glad to see me, offering concern, comfort, and support. They allowed me to ease back into my job, working harder for me than they ever had. Our friendship was very deep; they wanted only to make it as easy as they could, knowing it was overwhelming for me to try to get my life back together.

As the days went by, I started feeling physically stronger, but still mentally destroyed. It was difficult for me to hear talk about other children or to see pictures of babies.

It was also especially hard for me to be in any kind of crowd or party. Before my life changed, I had loved going out, being at parties, and socializing with people; now I became anxious, nervous, and sick to my stomach. It was so difficult for me to carry on any kind of conversation that I finally decided not to go anywhere. I found that I had talked about Louis so much for so long that now I didn't know how to have any kind of conversation that excluded him. People felt awkward around me, and if I met someone new, I was at a loss when asked if I had any children. I just couldn't tell them my son was dead.

The fear, depression, and anger manifested itself in other ways. Crossing the street became another nightmare for me. There were days when I would literally freeze, my heart racing at the thought of crossing the street if there was any kind of traffic. To this day, I still have that fear; time has diminished it somewhat, but it's always in the back of my mind.

However, the hardest question for me to answer or be asked is still, "Do you have children?" Of course I do, or I did, but he was killed. How do you answer that question without explaining a story you don't want to tell, don't want to relive, and don't want to repeat? Even six years later, that is still the one question I hesitate to answer. Sometimes I am at a loss for what to say.

My doctor put me on antidepressant pills, pills for the pain in my stomach, and sleeping pills for the nightmares that plagued me every night. I often wondered why doctors couldn't have discovered a pill you could take to make you forget all your bad memories.

Many unexplainable things have happened since we lost Lou. My sister Gloria had an experience at the exact location of the accident that certainly fits into that category. She had bought a piece of land, and was building a house several towns away. The location of the land forced her to travel past the site of the accident when she went there and when she returned. Every time she went by the site, she would try to fight the tears, and would softly talk to Lou about how much she missed him and how she hoped he was in a better place and at peace.

On this particular day, she was headed home as usual. As she came close to the location of the accident, she felt very lightheaded, and it increasingly got worse the closer she got to the actual scene. She felt a strange feeling going through her body, as if she had no control, and she felt the need to pull off onto a small street near the accident site. She finally pulled her car over and tried to regain control of herself, but to no avail.

She felt such a strange feeling inside and such lack of control that she began to think she had a serious medical issue. She called a friend using her cell phone, told her that she didn't feel well, gave her the location, and asked her to come for her if she didn't call back in fifteen minutes. Her friend felt a chill go through her body when she told her where she was.

When she hung up the phone, Gloria said she felt an extremely hot "wave" going through her body, starting at the top of her head and moving down very slowly. She could put her fingers on the location, following where it was at any moment. It traveled slowly down her entire body until it reached her feet, and then, suddenly, it was gone. As quickly as it came, it disappeared, and within minutes, she felt physically fine, but mentally drained.

She called her friend back and told her she felt well enough to drive. As she drove home, she wondered what had happened. She had never felt anything close to that feeling before, and she somehow knew that she probably never would again. As with Kevin, it took some time before she could verbalize to anyone what had happened, yet she still could not explain it. Although she didn't say it for a long time, deep inside, she knew Lou had made his presence known to her in hopes of somehow comforting her each time she had to make the trip up to the house.

As I tried to pick up the pieces of my shattered life, the world around me continued to revolve as if nothing had happened. Still, I grieved every day. I missed Lou's calls at work; I missed his presence in the house. Getting up every day for work was difficult, but in many ways, it was also my salvation. Every night after work, I would go to the cemetery before going home.

Tony and I were still together at this point, but our relationship was naturally strained. At night, he would come over; I'd cook dinner, and then have a few drinks. We'd watch television until I got tired, and then we would go to bed. This was my life, and I was miserable.

My family tried to be supportive, but how can you possibly hope to fill the black hole of pain and despair that is left behind in the wake of a child's death? My father, for instance, would give me cards with little poems written in them when I went over. He had been devastated when Louis had died. They had gotten close over the years and used to play basketball together in my backyard. He attended the wake, but left during the funeral mass, because he was sick, but also because it was too painful for him to bear. He wanted to help me so much, but he didn't know what to do.

I described my days as "bad days" and "worse days." Gone from my vocabulary was anything even remotely resembling a "good day." I had an appointment to see my lawyer. He needed to appoint an executor for my son's estate, not that Lou had anything except bills and a truck to pay for, but legal formalities required my signature. Once I arrived, my lawyer informed me that, true to form, my ex-husband had come forward to make that claim himself. I had paid all the bills incurred from the wake and funeral, borrowing money from my parents, because my ex-husband, in his words, "had no money" and never offered to help pay for anything, but here he was trying to receive any money the driver's insurance company would be paying for the loss of my son.

I called it "blood money." He called it "a new car." So three months after my son's death I would be in court for two cases: one against the boy who had killed my son, and the other to fight for the right to be the executor to a son whom Michael and I had raised. This would be one case my ex-husband would not win, and I would make sure of it. Both cases together would last eight months and would end just before the first anniversary of my son's death.

I put all my energy into getting better. I started working out again, gradually rebuilding my muscles and using the treadmill for my cardio workout. I knew I would need to stay healthy for the months ahead, and I forced myself to go to the gym at least four days a week. Sheer will and determination found me once again pushing myself to survive the coming months ahead. Years later, I would look back at that first year with such devastation and pain, but it was also the year of my transition into another world—a world I would become a part of for the rest of my life.

Tony became one of my reasons for living. The endless days and nights following my son's death now became his nightmare as well. As I started drinking more at night, he watched helplessly, not knowing how to comfort me. I found that drinking numbed me enough to sleep through the night without pain. Some nights I became angry and hostile; other nights I would feel totally helpless, and cling to him.

If given the choice, I'm sure he would rather have been somewhere else with someone other than me. I loved him, but when Louis died, it was all I could do to survive. My feelings for Tony were pushed aside. Pain and grief replaced all other feelings for anyone and anything. My feelings at the time were like a sharp, jagged knife puncturing my heart every minute of every day, destroying my soul—destroying me.

My house had become a shrine to my son. I had always hung pictures of him on the walls; school drawings and things he had made at school were either on the refrigerator or in my office at work. Now, every room was filled with so many more pictures that I had started taking down wall decorations to make more room for them. I needed to see his face in every room.

I had left his bedroom alone, exactly as he had left it, with his clothes still in the drawers. I shut the door, and his room remained the same, as if he had just gone out. On nights when he had come home late, he would come into my room, let me know he was home, and then go into his room, shut the door, and fall asleep. Time stood still in his room, and that's exactly what I wanted.

On nights when I couldn't sleep, I would go into Lou's room and fall asleep in his bed. It was often comforting, but emotionally draining. I'd open my eyes, see all the familiar things around me, and then realize he was never coming home again. He would never walk through that door again. I punished myself unmercifully, but it was something I needed to do—something I wanted to do.

I lived in misery and continued to deprive myself of anything good that came my way. And although I kept his door shut, over the next five years, whenever I came home, the door would be open. I'd immediately walk down the hall and shut it. Then, during the days when Tony and I were home, the door would just open. I'd hear it, and walk down the hall and shut it, only to have it happen over and over again over the years. I got so used to it that when I'd walk into the house, the first thing I would do would be to shut his door. It became a habit; I never questioned it. Like so many things that happened during that time, it just...*was.*

I had felt his presence in the house for so long that it no longer bothered me, but it did bother people who came over. So Tony replaced the door's frame and changed the doorknob, but nothing worked. The phone would ring at three in the morning, and when I picked it up, there would be nothing but the dial tone. Sometimes the doorbell would ring early in the morning; I would get up, and no one would be at the door. Tony never heard either the phone or the doorbell, so I accepted the fact that I was just going crazy. This would continue to happen for years, until a series of miracles would finally end my descent into darkness.

As winter turned to spring, it was decided that Easter Sunday would be held at my twin's house. We had each picked out a holiday to have family over for dinner so my mother wouldn't have to cook every time. I had picked Christmas, which I had every year until my son died. Mike had Easter, and my mother had Thanksgiving.

The holidays were the worst times of the year. While everyone was being thankful for what they had, I longed for what I didn't have. As much as I tried, I couldn't even pretend I wanted to be there. The night before Easter, I had washed a load of laundry. As I took the clothes out to put them into the dryer, I felt something at the bottom of the washing machine. I couldn't see anything, but I felt something small. As I picked it up and looked at it, I realized it was a tiny Easter Bunny earring. I reached down and found another one. I held them both in my hands. They weren't mine. I had never seen these earrings before, and had never even owned anything like them.

I showed them to Tony, and he didn't recognize them either. Where had they come from? I knew, but Tony said nothing. As much as he wanted to believe, he just couldn't. Then I started to cry, knowing somehow Louis had sent me an Easter present. There was simply no other explanation. It was then that I started to realize he was reaching out to me, and in my grief, I couldn't realize the extent of the love he was sending to help me survive. So I started receiving gifts, in one form or another, that would force me to believe in the afterlife.

I would tell my family, and even show them my little gifts, gifts I couldn't explain, but I knew they felt there was some other reason for them, a logical reason they would be able to understand. The more they disbelieved, the more distant I became. My bond with my son was so strong that sometimes, when he was growing up, I had felt we were one person. I couldn't explain how I knew these gifts were from him; only time would be able to prove it. My family felt I was definitely going crazy, and all they could do was watch helplessly as I pushed them away and lived in my own private hell.

As Mother's Day approached, I wished my friends a happy Mother's Day weekend as I left. The look on their faces said it all. What could they say to me on this, my first Mother's Day without the son I had mothered? I felt their sorrow at knowing how hard the weekend would be for me. True friends forever: that's what I call them, and that's what they were. On Mother's Day, I woke up with a huge emptiness in my heart; I didn't want to wake up at all. All I wanted was peace. Tony had bought me roses and a card. On opening the card, I saw that he had written, "You will always be a mother, Louis would have wanted you to have these flowers."

Tony was so thoughtful. He was always caring, and tried to help me with my nightmare, yet it was agonizing for him at the same time. As I sat down and cried with the flowers in my hands, I knew I truly loved him, but I just wasn't able to show him how much. I felt paralyzed. I felt guilty whenever I felt a moment of happiness.

Louis's birthday was May 28. He would have been twenty-two. It was an intensely painful and gut-wrenching time for me. Flowers were finally starting to bloom at the cemetery, and I brought down a dozen pink and white roses to place on the headstone. Then I celebrated his birthday alone, planting even more flowers.

I had decided not to open my pool that summer. My son's birthday had always been celebrated on Memorial Day weekend with the opening of the pool, followed by a big cookout. It was just like the holidays that had come and gone; I didn't wish to bring up another painful memory. My friend Scott from our morning "breakfast club," who had always offered so much support, concern and help, said, "You have to open the pool; it's going to be the hottest summer on record."

I had to laugh at that one. Scott also had a pool, and our summer conversations always included pool activities, the planting of flowers, and cookouts. So once again, to try to bring some normalcy to my life, I opened the pool in June, and, just as he'd predicted, it was a long, hot summer.

As the days went by, I was in and out of court in Milford for the pending trial of my son's death, and in Worcester fighting for the right to be the executor of my son's estate. Each court appearance took more and more out of me. I had started to put on a little weight, and working out had finally returned muscle to my arms and legs. I weighed only a hundred and ten pounds, but I *looked* healthier, even if I didn't feel it.

One Saturday in early July, my father was sitting by the pool with me. Whenever he saw me outside, he would walk over and sit on one of the chairs, have a few beers, and just talk. He had never gotten over Louis's death and had aged quite a bit. He wasn't feeling well, and he was scheduled to go into the hospital that Monday to get his heart regulated. He had arrhythmia of the heart, which translates into an irregular heartbeat, and needed to have a shock treatment to regulate it. It was an outpatient procedure, so fortunately he would be home the same day.

He had been a heavy smoker and had been told ten years earlier to quit smoking and drinking, which he had done, but he had still developed emphysema. As we sat and talked, he had a few beers, something he had started again after Louis had died. I wished him luck on Monday as he left. Monday night after work, I went to see him. His blood pressure was high, and he had developed a cold, so they would have to wait until he was better to shock his heart. He refused to have the television on, and as I sat there talking with him, he looked at the black screen. I knew all too well what that felt like; sometimes staring at nothing at all was better than seeing the concerned faces of those you loved.

One afternoon, I walked into his room. He was sleeping, so I just sat there and waited for him to wake up. He had been in the hospital for five days by then, and he had lost weight and appeared very pale. It was the first time I saw my father look frail and old. Once he woke up, I gave him his coffee frappe and talked about nothing—just made conversation to pass the time. By the following Monday, he was strong enough to have his procedure, and he came home that afternoon. My sisters, brother, and sister-in-law went over on Monday to welcome him home. On Tuesday night, he appeared to be a little better, but was having trouble breathing, so we installed an air conditioner in his bedroom. It was hot and humid, a typical July week in New England. Mike and I stayed with him for a while, and then we went out and had coffee with my mother.

As we talked, my father called out to my mother, so she left us to attend to him. When she came out, she said that he wanted to know if the twins were still here. So Mike and I went in, and my father said, "You know, I would really like a strawberry sundae." Eager to please, Mike and I went to the Dairy Queen that was just five minutes from the house and brought one back for him. It was the last thing my father ate.

At eight-thirty on Wednesday morning, my mother called me at work to tell me my father had died early that morning of a heart attack. The ambulance had just taken him to the hospital. I told her I would meet her there. As I hung up the phone, I stared out the window for a few minutes, saying a silent prayer. Then I picked up my pocketbook, told Stephanie, my associate, that my father had died, and drove to the hospital to be with my family.

On the way, I thought to myself, *I can't go through this again so soon after Louis has died. I just can't take it.* It had only been eight months; I wasn't ready for another death, especially my father's. My brother, Kenny, met me in the hall at the hospital. Joanie and my mother were in a private room, and I walked in and hugged them both. I asked Kenny where my father was, because I needed to say good-bye to him. Kenny said that it might not be a good idea, but I insisted. I had always felt guilty that I had not been able to say good-bye to Charlie when he had been killed. I had lived with that guilt for twenty-five years, always feeling that I should have seen him one last time; maybe then I could have found some kind of peace, instead of living with that unspoken farewell.

I couldn't live with that feeling for my father. Kenny took me to the room where my father had been brought. As I stood there looking at him, my thoughts went back to Louis. He had looked so peaceful in his final moments, like he had just fallen asleep. This was different. The paramedics had tried to bring my father back, but had failed. It was obvious: my father looked like he had fought to stay alive. What I saw in that room was how I would remember him for the rest of my life.

I walked out and told Kenny not to let Mike or Gloria see him like that. It was a moot point; by the time they arrived, they had already decided not to see him. They wanted to remember him as they had seen him the night before. Tony had arrived while we waited for my sisters to come. We stayed there for a while to be close to Dad, and then left to prepare for another wake, another funeral, and heartache.

When Louis was growing up, my father had told him he could have his wedding ring once he had died. As I walked into my mother's house that day, I went into my father's room, picked up his wedding ring, and put in on my right hand. I walked out the back door, across the lawn, and into my house to grieve by myself before the family came over to offer their support while we made the final arrangements.

The wake and funeral were held at the Consigli-Ruggerio Funeral Home, and it was déjà vu all over again: the same place where Louis's funeral had been held. Once again, David was compassionate, caring, and professional, guiding us through the wake and funeral with such ease that we were able to concentrate on our grief and the support of family and friends.

At the funeral mass, I went up and read a poem for my father. Although devastated over his death, I found I had not been able to cry when my mother told me he had died, and it had bothered me enormously. I had cried so many tears for my son that I literally had no tears left.

After the funeral, I fell into another deep depression and started drinking even more at night. My one consolation was living next door; I had been able to get close to my father and had finally been able to break through the silence of years gone by. My sisters and I had finally been able to have fun with him, always asking who his favorite was. We would tease him on the phone by saying "This is your favorite daughter," and he would try desperately to figure out which one it was before saying a name.

Sometimes he would call us at work and play the song, "I Just Called to Say I Love You." He would hear it on the radio, and dial one of our numbers, and we would have to listen to the whole song. It was his was way of telling us he loved us without having to say it himself. I wasn't alone in my grief; his death affected my sisters terribly.

Mike would go up to the house every Thursday and have lunch with him. He waited faithfully for her every week. It became their "quality time." I would often call on those days to talk to him, just as a joke, and Mike would hang up on me. Gloria was always his "baby." Since she was the youngest by eleven years, he had been able to spend more time with her as she grew up, and had doted on her every day. She became the "princess." Once again the family grieved, this time for my father's death and for the loss we had suffered over the past eight months. At least I knew he was now with Louis, and I hoped he was finally at peace.

As summer turned to fall, I dreaded each court session I had to attend. I had already been to court in Worcester twice for Louis's estate and twice in Milford for my son's death. In the end, my ex-husband and I were awarded the position of joint executors of Louis's estate. The court case against the boy who had killed my son dragged on, and when the final hearing was held, the case was dismissed, and the death of my son was called an accident.

Thankfully, the court had spared me the anguish of having to appear as a witness. But as the police read the witness reports in court, I sat there with my family and listened to the horror of his accident yet one more time. As I walked out of court with Tony and my family, the boy on trial called out my name.

I turned around and looked at him, and he walked over and hugged me, telling me how sorry he was. His gesture both surprised me and caught me off guard.

Someone else might have just walked out of court. However, this boy had the decency and respect to tell me once again how sorry he was, not knowing what my reaction would be.

I could have appealed the judge's decision, knowing I probably would win if the case was presented before a jury, but I didn't. It would not have brought my son back, and I knew I couldn't go through it again. I suppose that, deep down; I knew it had been an accident all along. The boy hadn't been drunk or on drugs, and more importantly, he had treated the ordeal over the last year with respect. I also knew that he had suffered deeply for his mistake, a mistake he would live with for the rest of his life. We both had lost enough: I had lost my son, my life, and my future; he had lost himself.

It had been the worst year of my life. I had lost my son and my father and survived two court cases, all in the space of a year. Now I was finally able to do what I had wanted to do since the night of my son's accident: I slit my wrists and tried to put an end to my suffering.

A coward's way out, I know, but life was truly a pain I could no longer live with. Tony and I went out one night, I drank too much, and when we got home, I went into the bathroom. Tony must have realized something was wrong, so he opened the door and found me bleeding. I couldn't even do *that* right. I hadn't gone deep enough—just enough to keep them bleeding.

As Tony wrapped up my wrists, he was totally disgusted; there would be no sympathy from him. He was just disgusted by how weak I was. He was so angry that he barely spoke to me for days. My family never found out until later, when I finally told them. I picked myself up once again and forced myself to live a life of which I wanted no part.

As Thanksgiving approached, Tony said we were going away for the week; it was going to be a surprise. He knew that the first anniversary of my son's death would be difficult for me; now he wanted to do something to ease the pain, or at least take my mind off of it.

My family, always very protective, insisted that he tell them where he was taking me, but he just laughed and said he'd call once we got there. We ended up going to a horse farm with an inn in New York. I had always loved horses, and had owned one for a year when I was nineteen. The week included unlimited riding. It was one of the best surprises I had ever had.

I enjoyed riding every day, and spending time with the owners, our riding guide, and his family. But the best part was that we were the only ones there on that long weekend. Tony took a lot of pictures of me riding and with the horses. It was a wonderful week, and the first time I felt somewhat normal.

When we got the pictures back, I looked at the ones of me riding my horse, and for the first time in a year, I saw a smile on my face that had disappeared after Louis died. My love of horses had put that smile back on my face. Unfortunately, it would prove to be the only time I was able to see that smile for a long, long time. Even so, I hung the pictures everywhere, just to remind myself that I could really be that person again.

I went back to work, continued working out, and tried to pull my life together so that I could at least get through Christmas, my birthday, and New Year's Eve. Although my relationship with Tony was still strained, he tried harder to understand me, and I tried harder to keep my distance, not wanting to lose someone else I loved.

As the holidays approached, I kept my Christmas decorations in the cellar. I had decided not to decorate my house. When Louis was alive, he had always picked out the Christmas tree, and then we would decorate it together. Now it was just me, and there was no reason to celebrate. We had Christmas dinner at my mother's house, and then our birthday cake in front of the Christmas tree. When New Year's Eve arrived, we didn't celebrate. There was no need, because, well, after the first year, you pick up the pieces and go on. Amazingly, I had survived a year more painful than anything I could have imagined. I had learned more than I ever cared to know about pain, grief, and the capacity to bear them.

So I suppose I did celebrate New Year's Day that year after all: I thanked God that I had been able to get through the year, forgetting that after the first year comes the second.

2000–2003

The second year of Louis's death was no easier than the first. I still existed, I still grieved, and the pain was just as devastating. I had become closer to Tony's sister, Anne, who by now had given up on even asking me how I was doing. All she had to do was to look at me to know there had been no change. Although I found talking about Louis extremely difficult and painful to other people, with Anne, it was almost comforting. She always offered to listen while I babbled on about my pain and suffering.

Nicole had also become an important part of my life. Seeing her brought back happier times of Lou's life, and we became closer than we had been when Louis was alive. While life continued, in my heart, time stood still. There was never a day that I didn't ache to hold my son or a day that wouldn't start with thoughts of him and end with hope for a better day, hope that the stabbing pain in my heart would lessen. But it never did, because deep down, I refused to let it.

In some sick way, I wanted to feel pain. My son had died, so how could I feel any other way? It became a difficult time for my family and Tony. They thought I'd had enough time to grieve, having suffered and grieved so much, but they couldn't understand what I needed in order to help me. Joanie would always bring over flowers or bring them to the cemetery, cheering me up for a moment. We shared an especially close relationship, and she also grieved and often cried for the loss of my son. I was drinking more every night, and there came a point where they were very concerned for my well-being. My relationship with Tony was still difficult.

We had good days and bad days. He was always on edge, hoping to say the right things, hoping to bring me back, to keep our relationship going, but what I really needed from him, he couldn't give. He needed to understand how deeply I was suffering, that I had become a different person and taken on a different personality, and that was who I would be from now on.

Did I like the person I had become? It didn't matter; I had no choice but to accept it. Life was different, and it had taken on a new meaning for me. Gone was the carefree girl he had known who was always smiling and so sure of herself. Now I was always depressed, angry, and hurt, and damn it, I just wanted my son back. No one knows the depths of sadness and pain parents who have lost their children feel. It is a pain like no other—totally indescribable and crippling. Outsiders can never enter that world, because they don't understand; they have never experienced this type of loss. The saying "walk in my shoes for just one day, and then you'll understand" was appropriate, yet unrealistic.

To keep busy, I started putting a video of my son together. I had taken thousands of pictures of him growing up, so I divided the video into three stages: his infant years, his teen years, and his adult years. I chose only the happy pictures of him, and every picture brought up so many painful yet beautiful memories. I would often sit on the floor and cry as I decided which ones to use. After several trips to Morin's Studio in Milford to consult on the types of pictures, words, and music to use, the end result from the studio was a beautiful tribute to my son and a keepsake I will have forever.

Work was going well, and already strong friendships were deepening as I leaned on my friends for comfort and support. I even went out to dinner on different occasions, hoping to enjoy myself, but I'd always leave early. I got tired easily, and the eight hours a day of putting on a smile were exhausting for me.

One night in early April, my twin asked me if Tony and I wanted to go to Florida and spend Mother's Day week at their time-share in Orlando. Of course I jumped at the chance, and I decided to take two weeks off. They would be staying for one week, and we would stay on for a second.

On Mother's Day, Tony took me to Sea World. We walked around the park, and Tony went over to one of the booths and started shooting basketballs. He couldn't miss. Every basketball he threw went in. Finally, the man in charge said, "Enough! Pick out whatever you want." As I looked at all the stuffed animals, I saw a giant Garfield looking down at me. It was the only one there. Tony gave it to me, and said, knowingly, "Happy Mother's Day." It was another gift from my son. I went home happy and carried Garfield on the plane with me, not taking the chance that the airlines might lose it.

As summer approached, we decided to spend a week on the Cape at my sister's house in Sandwich. Tony thought the ocean and salt air would be good for me. One beautiful hot afternoon, as the tide started going out, Tony said, "In a few hours we can get some sand dollars." I had been at the Cape many times, but I had never found anything but shells. As we waded in the water, we walked down a stretch of the beach. I started looking for the sand dollars and finally said to Tony, "I'll never find one." Then a memory flooded my mind of a time my mother, Louis, and I had been trying to catch crabs with a net. Louis had kept trying, but finally looked up at me and said, "I'll never catch any."

I had looked at his little sunburned face, with eyes as blue as the ocean. He had been wearing his navy blue hooded shirt. I had said, "I know you're going to catch one; I can feel it." He had looked back in the water and put his net in, and then he'd started saying, "Mom, I caught one!" He had been so excited that he couldn't stop. I had reached for his pail as he dropped them in, one by one, until the pail was filled. That night my mother and Louis had spent hours picking the meat out of the claws.

Now here I was, saying the same thing to Tony. As I walked farther out in the ocean, I felt something with my foot as the tide went back out. It was a sand dollar. I yelled to Tony, and he just smiled. Then I looked down, and they were all around me. As I bent down to pick them up, in the back of my mind I heard a voice say, "See, Mom? I told you." The roles were now reversed. Once again, I felt the same feeling of love fill my heart as when my son's beautiful little face had been looking up at me, when his net had been full of crabs.

One time, we went on vacation to Aruba, and a white dove was perched on our balcony every single day of our two-week trip. On another vacation in St. Martin, on our first night there we went to the casino; I played Louis's age on the roulette wheel and won three hundred and fifty dollars. It was almost like Louis was saying, "Have a great time, Mom!"

As I worked toward rebuilding a new life that I could survive in beyond the loss of my son, I realized my healing had only begun. It would take years for me to learn how to live in this world again and be able to say, and truly mean it, that I had survived. As the days, weeks, and months passed, I fought desperately to sort out my pain and put it somewhere that was tolerable.

On some days I would be fine; on others, I would feel like nothing had changed at all. Everything had a different meaning now. Things I had worried about before—work, relationships, and people—took on a life of their own. Things that had mattered so much no longer had the same meaning. The loss of my son was just too much to bear all at once, so it lingered quietly, but always present, in the years that followed his death.

I welcomed days that were better than others, but they never managed to last. I'd fall down, pick myself up once more, and wait. Each time left a bruise deeper than before. And over the next few years, I would realize and begin to acknowledge the depth of my loss. I expected my family, Tony, and those closest to me to help, but when they tried, I fought back, not realizing that I was the only one who could help me.

I had shed many tears, and I realized that they were not only for me, but also for Louis, who had lost his chance at life. I went through so many changes over the next three years that it was hard to place them. I got a tattoo of a teardrop with Louis's name underneath, an angel on my shoulder, a dove on my lower back, and finally LOUIS on my left ring finger. Then I got a navel ring.

With all the sudden changes, my twin thought I was going through what she called my "third childhood." I wasn't sure what I was experiencing. I had become someone different, and as I tried to live as that person, it became very unsettling to Tony and my family. I just didn't care. I did what I wanted. I had earned that right.

My faith in God had been challenged, and I was still angry that he had taken my son from me. As each year ended, another one began. The years flowed together, and I stayed in the same place for five years. I went to the cemetery every night on the way home from work. Every year on the anniversary of Louis's death, I would take off work and sit in the house for the entire day, always thinking the same exact thing: *If he calls this time, I'll be home to pick him up.* It was a ritual I had created, punishing myself every year for not being home for his first call that night so long ago.

I had been transferred to Marlboro, and spent the next two years working on staff assignments. I missed my friends terribly, but knew it was again time to move on. We kept in touch and went out to dinner once a month, catching up on each other's lives. I finally felt I could be on my own, no longer leaning on their shoulders to stay up. As the year went on, however, I started getting depressed again, often crying at different times during the day for no reason.

The few close friends I had made noticed the change, and when it became too much for me, I went back to my doctor. I explained what was going on, telling her that I didn't think my medication was working and confessing that I was becoming depressed again. She explained that I was going through something known as post-traumatic stress disorder, or PTSD. I had all the symptoms, including flashbacks, difficulty concentrating, and a feeling of detachment, so she changed my medication and hoped time would sort things out. After a few weeks, I did start feeling much better. I hoped that I wouldn't fall again, because my body was finally tired. I was tired of feeling grief.

I started making some changes in my life during the end of the fourth year. I took my mother to church on Mother's Day, and it became "our time" each year to do this together. I stopped drinking hard liquor. All I drank, when I wanted to drink, was wine. Tony was happy with that decision, to say the least. It had become almost a punishment to me (and others) when I drank. Drinking no longer helped me sleep peacefully at night, and most of the time I would get nasty and lash out at everyone around me. Tony had been so good to me over the years, making sure the holidays were special, buying me beautiful presents, trips and weeks on the Cape in the summer. I needed him to know how much I had appreciated him; now I could start to show him. The summer of 2003 became the turning point in my life. Although I didn't know it then, it would change my life forever.

An Angel in Disguise

That summer, my cousin Lynn, who was living in Florida at the time, came home to visit. We had always been close growing up, but we had lost touch, each of us going our separate ways. She came over to my house one day, and we tried to catch up on all the years of separation. We spent the day in the pool, and she brought me up to date on her business, a book she was writing, and various televisions shows she had been on. Most important was how she had achieved all of this.

As we swam and lounged in the sun, she told her story. Lynn had moved to Florida when she found living here had become so difficult that she needed a new beginning. It had turned out to be the beginning of a life she never could have imagined. Once in Florida, she had suffered through several abusive relationships and started to wonder why God had abandoned her. She had been full of sadness and pain.

After her divorce, she had been so broke that she had lived in a motel room with her three kids, a cat, and a dog. She had promised them and herself that she would not give up, and had been determined to find out what her passion in life really was. Eventually, she had gotten back on her feet. She had done some print modeling jobs for newspaper and hotel ads, and then got a lucky break and begun working as an investigator for a law firm.

After a few years, she had decided to go out on her own to reunite people with their lost children, parents, and grandparents. Once her work had started to become known throughout the state, she had expanded her business, Renuitepeople.com, on the World Wide Web and started working out of her home. Her business had become so popular that she had landed on *The John Walsh Show, the Iyanla Show, CNN Live,* Paramount Studio's *Life Moments,* and *Dr. Phil,* and had been featured in the Associated Press.

People had started calling and e-mailing her from all over the world. Lynn had been at the lowest point she thought possible. She had prayed to God to help her and believed so strongly that he had heard her prayers that her whole world had turned around. I was so proud of her and all she had accomplished that it was beyond words. Most important was the fact that her faith in God was stronger than ever. I realized that this was something I had lost after Louis had died.

She knew I would find my faith again. I wasn't so sure. I gave her a copy of Lou's video before she left, and we promised to keep in touch through e-mail and phone calls, which we did. I was proud to call her my cousin, and kept the articles from newspapers all over the world that she would send; eventually there were so many of them that I had to start a scrapbook just to keep everything together!

In the fall, a few months after Lynn left, the telephone company made an offer for early retirement. I had thirty-three years in by then, and I started to think seriously of leaving. I made copies of my retirement package and brought them to a financial advisor to look over. After a week, Tony and I went back to discuss my package. There was no question in my mind. My pension was much more than I had anticipated. I would invest it, take a year off, live on my severance pay, and decide what my next step would be.

I filed my papers the next day; I gave them to my supervisor and never looked back. I had spent more than enough time in the business world. It was time for me to do something else with my life—something different. What that was, I didn't know. However, I did know that there was something else out there for me to do. God had spared my life many times over the last thirty years, and I needed to know why. My retirement party was held on November 21, 2003, the night of my last day of work.

As the holidays approached, the sense of dread, emptiness, and pain arrived right on schedule, and on the fifth anniversary of my son's death I stayed home again and waited for the telephone to ring. It never did.

As I sat at the kitchen table, all of my yesterdays returned to haunt me. I stared at my son's picture, thinking how handsome he was. He would have been twenty-six this year. Where had the time gone? What would we have been doing now if he hadn't died? The radio was on, and as I listened to Whitney Houston sing, "I'll Always Love You," the tears fell from my eyes and I sobbed for the absence of Louis. All of a sudden the radio went off.

I felt an extreme feeling of peace that was unexplainable to anyone other than me. I felt Louis's presence in the room once more—the feeling I had felt so many times before, knowing my son was with me. I knew he wanted me to stop suffering and to move on with my life. I stood up, went over to the radio, and put it back on, but the song was over. But then again, so were my tears, and as I continued on with the day as I had for so many years, I couldn't help but think that the coming year might just be different, after all.

Thanksgiving was held at my aunt's house, and the next day, Tony and I went down to the Cape for the long weekend, as we had done the last few years. As always, it was a weekend I didn't want to be at home. Christmas and my birthday were spent at my mother's house. My twin and I celebrated our fifty-first year together, again with our birthday cakes and pictures taken in front of the Christmas tree.

As New Year's Eve approached, I made a promise to myself that I was going to make some serious changes in my life. Tony had been so wonderful over the years, and had gone through years of nightmares, personality changes, setbacks, anger, and grief with me. I needed to step back and look at myself through his eyes. When I did, I was amazed that he was still with me at all!

You expect your family to always understand and accept what you have become, but your boyfriend certainly doesn't have to. The months and years of roller-coaster rides were not worth the falls, at least not for him. I needed to make things right, no matter what I had to do. The sudden realization that I had changed so much over the years since Louis's death was almost too much to accept. What had become of me? I felt so old, and so tired of the person I had become. I didn't know her anymore, and I didn't want to know her. I had so few feelings left inside that I felt like a shell. I couldn't imagine what he really thought of me. Maybe he was hoping to get the old Pat back, and he had held on, hoping against hope that a miracle would happen—and one did.

In early March, my cousin Lynn called; it was a call that would change my life forever. As we talked, she said, almost casually, "Why don't you write a book on everything you have been through? You could help a lot of people; perhaps give them the help you could never find."

I thought about it for a few weeks, and then one day, I sat down at the computer and started typing, letting emotions that had been inside of me for thirty years flow onto the paper. I continued writing, more for therapy for myself at first, and then for all those people who had been through years of pain and grief and couldn't find help themselves.

As I completed each chapter, Lynn would always offer her support, encouragement, and confidence in me, which kept me going throughout the long months of writing. When I needed to stop and take a few weeks off because of the painfulness of the story, I would get discouraged, and she would always say, "Just wait until you're ready; it will come to you." And you know what? She was right. After a few weeks, I would sit back down at the computer and start typing again, picking up right where I had left off. It was a cathartic experience for me.

As spring turned to summer, Tony and I went down to the Cape again for a few weeks, bringing my mother and Tony's sister Anne with us. We had a great time, and I enjoyed the ocean, the salt air, and a sense of peacefulness I hadn't felt in years. Anne and I talked, and she knew I had finally changed. We celebrated the old Pat's return. My mother and Tony went fishing, and time flew by.

As fall approached, we closed up the pool and waited for the holidays to roll around once again. In November, as I sat at my computer, a few weeks before what would be the sixth anniversary of my son's death, I started crying. I was tired of the pain in my heart, and my body ached to release all the grief I had experienced for so long, always willing myself to feel the emptiness and heartache—that knife stabbing me over and over again, year after year.

I was mentally and physically exhausted. I had punished myself unmercifully. I wanted a life back. I needed to feel again. Then I did something I thought I had forgotten how to do: I prayed to Louis to give me some kind of sign that it was all right for me to let go. Then I prayed to God for the strength to do just that.

What happened next can only be explained as a series of miracles. The bracelet that Louis had given me so many years ago fell off. I felt his presence, and felt he was telling me to keep it off this time. I looked at it for several minutes, then walked into my bedroom and hung it next to his gold cross.

A few nights later, I dreamed I was standing at the cemetery with Louis holding my hand, and then suddenly he was gone. When I woke up the next morning, I finally knew what this dream meant: he didn't want me to keep going to the cemetery. I always cried when I was there, and it was so painful. Now he was telling me not to go—he wasn't there, he was in my heart and in my memories.

On the day after Thanksgiving, Tony and I went down to the Cape again for our long weekend. On, Sunday, as we headed down the highway to do some shopping, we saw cars swerving in and out of the lane. It was a main highway, and traffic was moving as fast as sixty-five miles per hour, then suddenly it started to slow down. We couldn't see anything ahead of us, and figured there was a dead animal in the road.

As we got closer, we saw something small and white running in and out of traffic. We finally realized that it was a dog and started to slow down. As I looked up ahead, I saw a truck approaching in the opposite direction. I knew that if we didn't do something, the dog would be killed. I screamed to Tony and opened the door of his Pathfinder. The truck swerved off the road to avoid hitting the dog, which ran across the highway under Tony's truck and jumped into my lap. It all happened in a matter of seconds. It happened so fast that I wasn't even sure *what* had happened.

I shut the door to the truck, unzipped my jacket, and put the dog under it, and then held him close. He was shaking uncontrollably, wet from the rain, and scared to death. As I held the dog close to me, I could feel his heart racing. There was no collar on him, he was covered with ticks and fleas, and I had the feeling he had been abused. We notified the MSPCA and also went online to check for missing dogs. Once we got him home, I brought him to the vet to see if he had a microchip to identify an owner, but all he found was fleas, ticks, and a severe ear infection.

As I looked down and saw his little face staring up at me, I felt an overwhelming sense of peace—a feeling that an enormous weight had been lifted from my shoulders, the weight of a lifetime of pain, grief, and sadness, all rolled up into one. And my heart filled with so much love for this little dog that it was beyond anything I had felt since Louis had died. Then I realized what the date was: I had buried my son exactly six years ago to the day. Was my son sending me one final gift, or was this just a coincidence? It was as if the sky had opened up and dropped this dog right onto my lap. I hadn't been able to save my son's life, but I had saved this dog's life.

Tony and I looked at each other, and he said, "I don't know what just happened, but this dog is lucky to be alive. What do you want to name him?"

I looked at him, grinned, and said, "You just said it: Lucky." I knew at that moment that I had to stop holding on and let my son go. How many signs did I need? I had asked for Louis's help, and I had asked God to give me the strength to let go, and they had both answered me. That answer had come in the form of a small white dog. We had saved each other's lives—a dog starving for love and affection, and someone who was now able to give him both.

It was time for Louis to leave and do God's work. I had let the pain and loss of my son claim six years of my life, a life I never chose for myself, but a life I would now be forced to live. Finally learning this had taken the death of my son: a loss I would never get over, and a loss that would be beyond anything else I would ever experience in my lifetime.

We will never forget what we have lost and the prices we have paid, but it's what we do with the time remaining in our lives that matters the most. If given the choice, would I give up everything I know now to have my son back? The answer would be, without a doubt, yes.

But that's just not a choice for me now. Louis will be forever in my heart. He may not always be the first thought on my mind when I wake up in the morning, but he will be my last one each night. For in my life, through all the pain and unhappiness, I was given the greatest gift of all: the love of a mother for her child.

I promised my son a lifetime of love, and that love will last until forever is gone. Hopefully, so too will the words in this book—a book that has seen me through the worst of times and brought me to the best of times. Through them all, I have always felt like someone else was guiding my hands as I wrote.

Thank you, Louis. Thank you.

Lucky

Epilogue

♦

All of My Yesterdays

"I liken my grief to the bird with a broken wing. She never soared so high again, but her song was so much sweeter."

—*Anonymous*

November 24, 2004:

As I stand here, in a place I've been a hundred times over the years, I reflect on my life, an echo running through all of my yesterdays, flashing back to a time when life was so different, so happy, and so full of promise. And as I think of the day I stood on that stage so many years ago, waiting to receive my high school diploma, I recall that it had been a day of happiness, but also a day of sadness.

I was glad that I would soon be choosing my own road to travel, yet at the same time, I experienced a wave of sadness at leaving my friends and memories behind. One door would close, but another would open.

I thought of a lost love, and the tragedy of a life taken so young. I thought of broken relationships, broken dreams, and failed marriages, and it was then that I realized I had never mourned for Charlie—not properly; not really.

I had simply chosen to move forward, to put him away in a place that would be safe, and as a result, I had lived in limbo for thirty years—thirty long and trying years. I had shut the door to my heart and had lived my life for all those yesterdays, forgetting that what really mattered was *today*. The answer had taken a long time for me to learn, yet I knew it was still soon enough for me to move forward, to step back into life, to open up my heart and let Tony back in.

I know I will never be the same person again. There has been too much tragedy, and too much damage. But I have learned that there is a time to grieve and a time to heal. I had the greatest love of my life, if only for a short time. At least I enjoyed it—every minute of it, every day. But it is finally time to say good-bye…for now.

My son will always be my greatest achievement, the greatest love of my life.

If I knew then what I know now, even with all the tragedy and heartache that was to come, I wouldn't have changed a thing. I still would have chosen the same road and lived my life the same way, if only to have had him in my life for the precious little time he was around.

And when my life is finally over, I know that we'll be together once more, and we will follow each other through each lifetime, just as we have in the past.

Just as I know Louis's smile will fill every sunrise for me through eternity.

As I placed the roses on the headstone, a slight breeze moved through my hair once again, but this time, I wasn't alone. Lucky stood beside me, with a look that told me it was time to leave.

And as I walked away, I turned my head just one more time and remembered a time when we were at the ocean, running along the sand, laughing as I picked you up, hugging you so tight, promising never to let you go—a promise I knew I would never break.

I love you, Louis: way past Jesus.

I felt it was important to add this poem at the end of my story. It is my interpretation of what I think Louis would have said as he looked down at me from heaven.

A Message from Heaven

When tomorrow starts without me,
And I'm no longer there to see,
If the sun should rise and find your eyes
Are filled with tears for me,
I wish so much you wouldn't cry,
The way you did today.
I know how much you love me,
As much as I love you,
And each time you think of me
I know you'll miss me, too.
But when tomorrow starts without me,
Please try to understand,
That an angel came and called my name
And took me by the hand
And said my place was ready,
In heaven far above,
That I'd have to leave behind,
All those I dearly love,
But as I turned to walk away,
A tear fell from my eye,
For all through life I'd always thought
I didn't want to die.
I had so much to live for,
So much yet to do,
It seemed impossible
That I was leaving you.
I thought of all the yesterdays.
The good ones and the bad,

I thought of all the love we shared,
And all the fun we had.
If I could relive yesterday,
Just even for a while,
I'd say goodbye and kiss you
And maybe see you smile.
But then I finally realized
That this could never be.
For emptiness and memories,
Would take the place of me.
And when I thought of worldly things,
I might miss come tomorrow,
I thought of you, and when I did
My heart filled with sorrow.
But when I walked through heaven's gate
I felt so much at home.
When God looked down and smiled at me
From his great golden throne,
He said, "This is eternity and all I've promised you,"
Today life on earth has passed,
But here it starts anew.
I promise no tomorrows,
But today will always last,
And since each day's the same day,
There's no longing for the past.
So when tomorrow starts without me,
Don't think we're far apart,
For every time you think of me,
I'm right there in your heart.

Louis
May 28,1977–November 24,1998

About the Author

✦

Patricia Forbes

Patricia Forbes grew up in the small town of Hopedale, Massachusetts. After graduating from high school, she worked for the telephone company for thirty-three years. In 2003, she retired to pursue other interests and decided to write this book: a story of healing and recovery.

Patricia has been accepted into the master's program of the American Academy of Grief counseling to work towards becoming a certified grief counselor. She enjoys horseback riding, working out, reading, and spending summers at the ocean. She lives in Hopedale with her boyfriend, Tony, and their dog, Lucky.

Patricia is currently working on a sequel to *Healing Life's Broken Dreams, From Darkness to Light*, which will be available in 2006. To visit her website go to www.lifeafterlouis.com.

978-0-595-35413-9
0-595-35413-0

Printed in the United States
36221LVS00005B/202-273

9 780595 354139